Fantasy Voices

Interviews with American Fantasy Writers

**Conducted by
Jeffrey M. Elliot**

R. Reginald

the Borgo Press

San Bernardino, California
MCMLXXXII

For Janine—
Who Makes Me Laugh and Feel Loved

CONTENTS

Abbreviations Code: JE—Jeffrey M. Elliot; MWW—Manly Wade Wellman;
    JN—John Norman; HBC—Hugh B. Cave; KK—Katherine Kurtz.
Photographs on page 64, clockwise from top left: Manly Wade Wellman (photo
    by E. B. Boatner); John Norman (courtesy of John Norman); Katherine Kurtz
    (photo by Joyce Muskat); Hugh B. Cave (courtesy of Hugh B. Cave).

Library of Congress Cataloging in Publication Data:

Elliot, Jeffrey M.
    Fantasy voices.

    (The Milford series : Popular writers of today ; v. 31)
    1. Fantastic fiction, American—History and criticism. 2. Fantastic fiction—
Technique. 3. Authors, American—20th century—Interviews. I. Title.
PS374.F27E4   813′.0876′09   80-22575
ISBN 0-89370-146-7 (Cloth, $8.95)
ISBN 0-89370-246-3 (Paper, $2.95)
                                                                    OCLC #6762077

Produced, designed, and published by R. Reginald and Mary A. Burgess, The
Borgo Press, P.O. Box 2845, San Bernardino, CA 92406, USA.   Printed in
the United States of America by Vic Torrey at Victory Press, San Bernardino,
California.   Binding by Jack Troy at California Zip Bindery, San Bernardino,
California. Cover and title page designs by Michael Pastucha.

First Edition———January, 1982

Fantasy
Voices
1

INTRODUCTION

Gather round, ladies and gents, gather round! Step in a little closer, if you please. Yessir, folks, what you have here is a unique treasure, a remedy for boredom, a balm for the senses—a sure-fire product guaranteed to delight, amuse and astonish!

You've all heard of them—those square things with numbered pages full of printed nouns and verbs and adjectives liberally sprinkled with punctuation. They're called *books*—and believe me, folks, this one's a real humdinger. You can't afford to miss it! . . . Hurry! Hurry! Hurry! . . .

What's that you say? Too much "hard sell" for you? Well, don't blame me, I'm just doing my job. The fellow who writes the Introduction is, purely and simply, a pitchman, not so far removed from the silver-tongued snake oil salesman in the battered top hat, hawking his wares from the flatbed of a carnival wagon.

It helps if you happen to be enthusiastic about your product. In my case, it's essential: I can't jump and dance around up here in front of the reader unless I happen to think that *this* particular bottle of snake oil or this particular book is damned good stuff!

Which is why, when Jeff Elliot asked me to write the introduction to *Fantasy Voices #1*, my initial reaction was negative. I scanned the contents, shaking my head. Four interviews, with Manly Wade Wellman, John Lange (John Norman), Hugh Cave and Katherine Kurtz. Nope. Can't write the intro. Sorry, Jeff, but thanks for asking. My reason for refusing was sound: I had not read the work of these four authors, so how could I stand up and tell the reader about how wonderful they were?

Oh, sure, many years ago, in the pages of *Fantasy and Science Fiction*, I'd read some of Wellman's fantasy tales of John the Balladeer (and enjoyed them), but I'd not read a word of Lange or Cave or Kurtz. I was about to mail my "no" letter to Jeff when, out of idle curiosity, I decided to sample some of the manuscript. Began one of the interviews—and couldn't put it down! Tried another. Same result. Read them all with fascination and mounting enjoyment. Four minds revealed. Four careers examined. Not a boring page in the lot.

"Look, Nolan," I told myself. "If you zipped happily through four interviews with four authors whose work you *don't* read—enjoying each—then this book will probably be *twice* as enjoyable to readers who *are* familiar with these authors!"

So I dumped my "no" letter and sat down to write this Introduction.

Before I go any further, let me acknowledge the pervasive influence of Jeffrey M. Elliot—a smart, tenacious, ubiquitous fellow who is rapidly becoming the Boswell of fantasy and science fiction. Perhaps I should refer to him in the plural, since I am convinced that there are at least four to six Jeff Elliots (cloned from one of his cells) hopping busily around the country interviewing scores of genre writers for scores of magazines and books. How else explain the fact that his bylines are legion in our time?

An Elliot here . . . an Elliot there . . . You're talking to him on the phone and the doorbell rings. Isn't that Elliot at your front door, a smile on his face, a sheaf of questions in his hand, tape recorder at the ready?

Jeff's doing us all a vital service, bringing the writers (whose work we love) to life on a page (see his *Science Fiction Voices #2*, with Bradbury, Niven, Anderson, van Vogt and Silverberg), asking the right questions, urging his subjects to share their lives and passions with us, allowing us all to get to know one another in this wide and wondrous world of fantasy.

Now, specifically, are the four individuals you're going to meet in this book all truly fine writers worthy of extended, in-depth interviews? I can't answer that because I *still* haven't read them. But does it really matter? The point is that all four have very interesting, fresh things to say about writing, their lives, their backgrounds—and about what I term "the human condition." They care about people, and you'll care about *them*.

Mr. Lange seems more than a bit annoyed by science-fiction critics who have attacked his best-selling "Gor" novels. Are the critics right, or is Mr. Lange right? Who cares? The fun lies in "listening" to what strong-minded Mr. Lange has to say about his novels, and about how and why he writes. (By the way, Elliot has managed a "scoop" here, since John Lange speaks about his work for the first time anywhere!) The man's a sheer delight. His "voice" is articulate, sharp and informative. So who cares what his "Gor" novels attract in pro or con criticism? Go read one and find out for yourself if he's any good. Maybe you'll hate the thing, or maybe you'll love it. But the *man* is great fun and that's what this book is all about.

Take Katherine Kurtz (and Lord help you if you call her Kathy!). Never met the lady, but I now feel I know her . . . know how her mind works . . . what her individual loves are (and who else in the genre wears medieval gowns and has served as reigning Queen in the Society for Creative Anachronism?) . . . She's terrific. Vital, enthusiastic, engaging. Are her novels any good? Don't ask me. I'm just up here to tell you that Katherine herself is a fascinating individual.

Hugh Cave is into voodoo. Deep into it. Knows plenty. And tells you about it. Informs you. Shares his specialized, hard-won knowledge. You won't be bored, I promise, as you "listen" to him in these pages. I may be doing Mr. Cave an injustice in stating I've never read him; he's been around as a pro for many years and no doubt I've encountered his work in the pulps, back in my high school days when I devoured whole issues of *Weird Tales*, like Clark bars, each month! Fantasy was my first love. (Long before I discovered science fiction, or dreamt of creating the Logan novels, I was an avid fantasy buff.)

Finally, we come to Manly Wade Wellman, another oft-published veteran who has been entertaining readers for decades. When I attended the last World Fantasy Convention, in Providence, Rhode Island, I met Manly at a late-night party in a crowded hotel room. He was sitting on the bed with two lovely young ladies and a guitar (an innocent scene, let me assure you!) and was singing folk ballads in his scratchy mountain voice. He had tears in his eyes as he sang of lost loves and Southern mornings, totally immersed in his world of authentic folk music. In fact, Manly wasn't in that hotel room; he was striding a narrow dirt road, guitar slung across his shoulder, deep in the Southern mountains. It was a sight to remember.

This is a book to remember—and Mr. Wellman's authentic voice is here "singing" to us in these pages; John the Balladeer is alive in him.

I've made my pitch. I've sold my snake oil.

Now it's time for you to open the bottle!

William F. Nolan
Woodland Hills, California
1981

MANLY WADE WELLMAN: BETTER THINGS WAITING

Perhaps more than anyone else, the writer must find what he is from within himself. For he is alone with himself, must understand himself and wield himself in all he writes.

Your life is measured, not by time or ability or knowledge or reputation, but by the work you do. Faulkner said, Get it done. Take chances. It may be bad, but that's the only way you can do anything really good. Hemingway said, Apply the seat of the pants to the chair and the fingers to the typewriter. Wolfe said, There can be no talent for writing whatever unless you have power to write. Hear all these things, but also hear yourself.

The road a writer follows is paved with words he writes. It may be long or short, wide or narrow. It is the only solidity on which his feet may travel. Every step forward on the road he makes goes into new, unborn country, full of wonders and perils and ecstacies he can dream of only as he encounters them.

It is never a royal road. Royalty rolls in chariots or is carried on the shoulders of slaves. Drudgery produces the words that pave your road. Nobody can give the words to you. You find and use them all by yourself, away from sight and sound of anybody you think might help.

What you find you must use. If you chew it too long in meditation, it becomes limp and lifeless. Remember the poet who knelt to thank God for an inspiration. When he rose from his knees, he had forgotten it.

Use everything. Don't hold back something for the next time. If it's good, if it fits, use it now and trust God, or whoever's up there pretending to be God, for more to use the next time. It is there when you need it. It always is. Inspiration never comes to you, it is there, a part of you, distilled from all you know and feel and dream and hope. It flows within you as your red blood flows.

But none of it is of any worth to you unless it is of worth to someone reading it. You don't know him. His face and eyes and mouth would be strange to you. But he must say to you, "I know what you mean and it is good, it is valid. It helps me, I'm glad I read it."

That's why you write in the Lonesome Valley, with only your thoughts like ghosts around you. For someone else, in some other valley, who reads you and believes you.

When you can't do it anymore, it's time to rest. Stop writing books and read them. Take two drinks every evening instead of one. You've come to the bottom of the hill. Maybe there'll be a soft place to sit.

—Manly Wade Wellman, 1975

Born in Portuguese West Africa (now Angola) on May 21, 1903, Manly Wade Wellman's roots reach far back into history, bridging the worlds of Colonial America and the Confederate South, with ancestral traces of Gascon French and American Indian. After his service in Africa, Wellman's father, a medical missionary, brought his family to the United States when Manly was still a young boy. During those early years, Manly lived in many parts of the country—Washington, D.C., Arkansas, Kansas, Utah—but never quite long enough in any one place to call it home. Like most boys his age, Manly loved to travel, and did so by hopping freights, on horseback, by car, and on foot. As a youngster, he held a wide range of part-time jobs, among them harvest hand, house painter, soda bottler, cowboy, and roadhouse bouncer (his favorite). In prep school, Manly distinguished himself on the football field, a talent which won him a scholarship to attend Wichita University (now Wichita State). After graduating with a B.A. in 1926, he went to Columbia University, where he received a B.Litt. in 1927. From there he returned to Wichita to work as a reporter for the *Beacon* and, somewhat later, the *Eagle*.

For as far back as he can recall, Wellman wanted to be a writer. As early as 1925, at the ripe young age of twenty-two, he found a market for his poetry, as well as short stories, all written while he was in prep school and college. Despite his success at writing, he received little encouragement from family or teachers, who tried to dissuade him from becoming a writer. One of his first stories, "Back to the Beast," prompted a teacher to remark: "Your work is impossible!" That story later found a home in the pages of *Weird Tales* (November, 1927), and was his first professional sale.

From 1927 to 1930, Wellman worked as a reporter in Wichita until a personal altercation with a "hungover editor," who made the mistake of cussing him out for something he hadn't done. Wellman promptly quit and turned to free-lancing on a full-time basis. This was a particularly bold decision, as it was the height of the Depression and jobs of any kind were hard to come by. Wellman, however, persevered, wrote whatever he was asked, and made it by on a shoe-string budget. In 1930, he married a music student, Frances Obrist, a Texan by birth, with whom he "ham and egged it" until better times came.

It was in this period that Wellman made his first foray into the science-fiction field, with several sales to the poorly-paying Hugo Gernsback chain. Indeed, Gernsback bought a number of his early tales, including *The Invading Asteroid*, a space-opera thriller, and the first of many novels to come. Clearly, though, Wellman could not make ends meet by writing for Gernsback at the "penny a word" rate he was getting. In 1934, hoping to improve his standing, he moved to New York in order to be closer to the markets. Although times were rough, he made a number of quick sales to the Macfadden chain, and then, in 1935, sold "Outlaws of Callisto" to *Astounding* for $150, a story that would later become one of his classic tales. This sale proved to be a major turning point in his career.

Although Wellman wrote prolifically and well in several fields, he remained, for the most part, a writer of science fiction and fantasy, at least until the end of World War II, when the bottom dropped out of the market. However, it was in the fantasy field that Wellman did his best writing, owing perhaps to his lifelong interest in the genre. During these years, he forged a close working relationship with Farnsworth Wright, of *Weird Tales* fame, for whom he wrote dozens of stories, and proved to be one of *Weird Tales'* most popular writers.

It didn't take Wellman long to crack all of the field's major markets, as well as most of its minor ones, selling numerous stories to *Unknown* and *Strange Stories*. His most famous fantasy series, though, appeared in *Fantasy and Science Fiction*, which published his popular stories of John the Balladeer, a wandering mountain minstrel who battled supernatural evil. These stories were later collected in *Who Fears the Devil?*, and served as the basis for a motion picture which bore the character's name.

In 1939, Wellman moved to New Jersey, accepting a job as managing editor of the Gold Medal syndicate. He quickly tired of the work, however, and joined up with Golden Age comic books, creating characters and writing stories for such well-known comic heroes as Captain Marvel, Blackhawk, Green Lantern, Captain America, Aquaman, Captain Midnight, and many others.

When World War II came, Wellman enlisted in the army, and served stateside as a first lieutenant. At its conclusion, he faced a critical career decision. Indeed, most of the major markets for which he wrote previously—pulps and comics—were on their last legs. Anticipating rough times ahead in the fantasy field, Wellman shifted his efforts to other areas of writing, chief of which were hardcover novels and nonfiction works.

In 1946, Wellman left New Jersey and moved to Pine Bluff, North Carolina, a move that satisfied his Southern instincts and upbringing. An ardent student of Civil War history, he saw the move as extremely promising in terms of future research. In 1947, Wellman published his first hardcover volume—*Find My Killer*—a highly popular mystery novel. He then turned his hand to writing juvenile books, a move which later resulted in several awards and citations. And then, in 1949, Wellman published *Giant in Gray*, his best-known biographical work. Based on his namesake, Confederate General Wade Hampton, the book served to win him a reputation as a first-rate Civil War historian.

Wellman moved to Chapel Hill, North Carolina in 1951, where he has continued to reside for the last thirty years. With that move, he extended his forays into mainstream and nonfiction writing, penning "A Star for a Warrior," which won the first Annual Ellery Queen Award (beating a story by Faulkner); *Dead And Gone*, which won the Mystery Writers of America Award; *Rebel Boast*, which was nominated for the Pulitzer Prize; and *Worse Things Waiting*, which won the World Fantasy Award.

Despite his popular success in the science fiction-fantasy field, Wellman virtually stopped writing his popular yarns with the demise of *Weird Tales* in 1954. He turned his attention, instead, to hardcover writing—juvenile books, mainstream novels, Civil War history, and regional history. He also taught classes in creative writing at the University of North Carolina and at neighboring

Elon College.

In 1974, Wellman retired from teaching. With more time to write, he decided to heed the mounting requests from editors who wanted new fantasy tales. His son, Wade, suggested that they collaborate on a series of Sherlock Holmes pastiches for *Fantasy and Science Fiction* (these were later collected into a book). Editor Jerry Page, of *Witchcraft and Sorcery*, urged Wellman to send him a new series (the Lee Cobbett series). And Wellman, who felt at home in his new mountain habitat, started writing stories about mountain people and their ways. Around this time, Carcosa Press published a collection of Wellman's best fantasy stories—*Worse Things Waiting*—which received high praise.

Karl Edward Wagner, one of the fantasy genre's premier talents and the publisher of Carcosa Press, has known Wellman for many years, both as a writer and friend. In a recent biographical essay on Wellman, Wagner summarizes his career and speculates about his future, stating: "The dean of fantasy writers has buckled his sabre and revolver back on, and after a long leave of absence has mounted up and ridden back into the field . . . Several new fantasy books and stories will be coming out in the next months. And they won't be his last. Wellman, still in his prime as a writer, has more novels and stories in production. He won't quit writing, won't quit what he calls the 'outlaw profession.' They'd have to shoot him first."

JE: Can you recall when you first thought about being a writer? Did you receive much encouragement from your family and teachers?

MWW: I don't know when I first wanted to write. As soon as I could read, I suppose. For many years, my mother kept a story I wrote when I was six. When I was in grade school, I'd write in study period when I should have been doing my arithmetic, and the teacher would take the stories away. In high school, all my friends would read my stories and say nice things. By the time I was in college, I was selling. Wanting to do this was like wanting to be a doctor or a preacher or a policeman with other boys. I come from a family of writers, but none of us got much home encouragement. Things were fairly economical, making the realities of food and clothing more pertinent. Also, I seemed to neglect my school work—I never did make exceptional grades. Only one or two teachers encouraged me; the others felt I was wasting my time. In any case, a writer must write alone, and had better get used to that truth.

JE: Why did you turn to writing as a full-time career? What needs did it serve?

MWW: I always wanted to be a writer. I sold my first stories when I was still in college. I worked for newspapers, and when I was out of a job at the bottom of the Depression, I'd already sold some things. I simply went full-time then, as I'd always wanted to do, and made it go. It was like running away from a bear; you know you can't, but you've got to, and so you do. Writing, as Jesse Stuart says, is the last independent profession. It's also a compulsion. I wouldn't do anything else. The need it serves is the sharing of experience and emotion with a reader—a stranger, who becomes your partner in what you tell.

JE: Were you driven to write or was it more a question of writing simply to make a living?

MWW: I was driven to write by an urge to write. I was as much urged to do that as someone else might have been urged to dive for sunken treasure, or preach to the heathen, or rob banks. What you grimly want to do, you more or less have to do. Psychologists call that being compulsive. Not that anybody pointed a gun and told me to write; quite the contrary. But I felt I had to write. Maybe I could have done well in some other profession, but I'm glad I didn't try.

JE: You've written both science fiction and fantasy. Do you prefer the latter genre? If so, why?

MWW: Yes. I prefer fantasy to science fiction. I can't keep up with science as I should to write about it. A scientific mind is needed for it, anyway. I'm fascinated by how science fiction becomes science fact. As for fantasy, maybe I've been deeper into it, thought more about it. But both genres appeal to the human sense of wonder.

JE: What is it about fantasy *per se* that makes it a productive area in which to work?

MWW: Fantasy writing spurs the imagination and the process of invention, takes you into world after world of wonder. You get fascinated with your own story as you tell it to yourself.

JE: What was the nature of the fantasy market at the time you began your career?

MWW: When I began, back in the 1920s, *Weird Tales* was the only fantasy magazine, *tout court*. Yet many magazines bought fantasy now and then. *Cosmopolitan* did, and *Everybody's, Argosy*, and others. The impulse of wonder was recognized. I tried to sell wherever I could, and once in awhile I succeeded.

JE: How was fantasy, as a literature, viewed by the public at that time?

MWW: In the bracket of society where I lived, fantasy was more or less viewed as a novel trifle. Those I knew took it seriously only when it was written by somebody with a thundering reputation, like Arthur Conan Doyle or H. G. Wells, or maybe hoary old classics by Edgar Allan Poe and Nathaniel Hawthorne. That was an era when admired Americans were men like Thomas Edison, Henry Ford, and Charles Schwab, none of whom wrote anything, just made money, which, President Calvin Coolidge and others assured us, was the *one* serious pursuit. Now and then somebody got a fantasy printed, but it bloomed to blush unseen, like the flowers in Gray's country churchyard.

JE: You've said that you owe your development as a writer to *Weird Tales*, and its pioneering editor, Farnsworth Wright. What role did Wright play in your early career?

MWW: Farnsworth Wright was tremendously patient with anyone he thought worth the effort. His criticism was painstaking and constructive. He had considerable education and appreciated nuances in writing.

JE: What was it about *Weird Tales*, as you suggest, that helped push you to your limits as a writer?

MWW: *Weird Tales* always made me feel like writing my best—giving them the best asparagus I had in the store—because it carried the sort of fiction I wanted to write. If you had any style at all, *Weird Tales* and its fine editor helped you develop it. The best authors in there were worth reading and admiring, and still are.

JE: You also wrote a number of stories for *Astounding*, until you split with its editor, John W. Campbell, Jr. What were your reasons for breaking with Campbell?

MWW: John Campbell was a successful editor, but he wanted mostly to give you germs of stories to write, and wasn't so apt to like your own ideas. We parted ways when he couldn't see what I was driving at when I wrote *Twice in Time*. And I was selling to other markets quite well at the time. I didn't think I needed him; I certainly didn't need his dictatorial manner.

JE: You knew many of the legendary writers and editors of the period. Could you share some of your impressions of men like August Derleth, H. P. Lovecraft, and Robert E. Howard?

MWW: Yes. I never knew Derleth face-to-face, but we had much friendly correspondence. He was an indefatigable worker—if he had worked longer on a story, he might have written fewer and better stories. He pestered me into gathering and revising *Who Fears the Devil?*, in which he had great and encouraging faith. I felt that he was a loss when he died, as a publisher, writer, and friend. Lovecraft, too, I never met. I was urged to write to him, but it seemed that you had to bow down to him, and I've never been good at that. His story, "The Outsider," was his first to grab me, and I still think it's a jewel. I'll repeat my thought that he, as much as any single person, made *Weird Tales* successful. As for Howard, I never met him. He remains to me a tragic figure. He had little opportunity for education or intellectual companionship. It's recognized now that he was strange in some ways. I've wondered if his insistence on being burly and two-fisted wasn't too much of a protest. I also wonder if his suicide may not have had more reasons than just the death of his mother; if he wasn't desperate in his effort to live by writing.

JE: To what extent was your writing influenced by Edgar Allan Poe? Can you detect the impact of M. R. James? What role did Lord Dunsany play? Did Lafcadio Hearn exert a major influence?

MWW: Influences on a writer are many. Everything he reads influences him. Poe was bound to be an influence; he virtually invented the atmosphere of the supernatural. I admire and constantly reread James, Dunsany, and Hearn. But I doubt if I write like any of them. I wish I wrote things as well as James did. In these writers, style is a precious jewel.

JE: Your most well-remembered fantasy series was *Fantasy and Science Fiction*'s "John the Balladeer." What explains the extraordinary appeal of these stories?

MWW: It isn't for me to say what makes people read you—if I knew that, I'd be far more successful than I am. The stories about John have succeeded most gratifyingly, have been praised and valued highly and embarrassingly. Perhaps that is because I did my best, and still do, to speak for the Southern mountains and their people, in their own language. Some have called these stories "poetic." If so, I'm not the poet. These natural men and women are the poets.

JE: Would you agree that the John stories represent your best writing?

MWW: I don't know what my best writing is. I've done a lot of mainstream fiction and nonfiction, and critics have mostly been kind. Whatever I happen to be writing at the moment is what I try to write best.

JE: You wrote an extremely intricate future history series—"The Thirtieth Century"—which spanned sixteen stories. Was it difficult to achieve consistency throughout the series?

MWW: Once I came to some decision on what the solar system would be like in the thirtieth century—not that it really will be like that—it wasn't truly hard to be consistent. I think I started with a notion of what Martians would be like—tentacled, chrysanthemum-faced—and something about their cities, Pulambar and Ekadome. I visualized reptilian Venusians, and colonists from the inner planets on what I chose to consider habitable moons of Jupiter. I kept sheafs of notes. I drew countless pictures of Venusians and Martians to help me out. Others, of course, have done this sort of thing, notably Robert Heinlein. But writing these stories was difficult. It's always difficult to write. It had better be, or the writing will be bad.

JE: Why did you turn your hand to writing for the comics? Did you enjoy the comics field? Was it challenging work?

MWW: Writing for comic books was easy and paid well. When I began, I wanted to buy a house so my family could have it when I went to the war that was on the way. I didn't particularly enjoy writing for the comics. In those days, they were mostly garbage. Anyway, I didn't write just comics. I was contributing to a number of magazines. As for challenge, I didn't recognize one very much.

JE: Who were your most memorable comics characters? What role did you play in developing Captain Marvel?

MWW: Most of the characters I did in the comics aren't memorable any more, except possibly as curiosa. I did Captain Marvel, but he was already a going concern. Others you may call to mind were Blackhawk, Plastic Man, the Spirit, and Aquaman. Some have to be forgotten—Fu Chang of Chinatown, Bentley of Scotland Yard, Green Lantern, the Jester, Ibis the Invincible, Spy Smasher, and Navy Jones. You'd better be living close to editors and go in for conferences before you wrote these scripts.

JE: Can you explain the now famous Fawcett/DC plagiarism suit involving Superman and Captain Marvel?

MWW: I believe that DC sued Fawcett, charging that Captain Marvel was plagiarizing Superman, because Captain Marvel was the *one* dangerous rival to Superman. He was humorous (Superman wasn't), and he was really a boy who turned into a hero by saying "Shazam!" Kids could, and did, identify.

JE: Was the sale of "Outlaws of Callisto" to *Astounding* a critical turning point in your career, particularly from a commercial point of view?

MWW: Yes. "Outlaws of Callisto" earned me $150 at the depth of the Depression. That was enough money to give me the time to think and plan other stories better. It was just as materialistic as that.

JE: It was recently reported that most of your early work has either been lost or destroyed. Is that true? If so, what happened?

MWW: I've lost a great deal of my early work, simply because the house isn't big enough for it. I've published seventy-two books and *circa* 500 magazine stories and articles.

JE: Why did you virtually stop writing fantasy and science fiction after the death of *Weird Tales*?

MWW: I stopped writing fantasy and science fiction because I was busy writing Southern history and regional fiction, with good book contracts. I stuck with *Weird Tales* to the end because of affectionate memories.

JE: What explains your fondness for pseudonyms, such as Gabriel Barclay, Levi Crow, Gans Field, Juan Perez, and others back then?

MWW: I used pseudonyms, usually, because back yonder I wanted a cent a word, at least, if I was writing under my own name. Gans Field was used at the suggestion of Farnsworth Wright—*Weird Tales* was using serials by me and might like to use Wellman stories in the same issue. Levi Crow was used on a series of Indian stories.

JE: Has your approach to writing fantasy changed significantly with the passage of years? Do you still experiment with new methods, new techniques?

MWW: By and large, I suppose I've always tried to tell simple stories, written as plainly as I can, in language I hope people can understand. If I've changed, it's by experience and by observation of life, literary and otherwise. I hope I've become better by diminishing old faults. I hope I'm not turbid and rackety, as once I was. Yet you have to be conditioned by good writing all around you. It helps you to write better. Some think of Poe's stories as quaint and somewhat old hat. But if Poe had kept on living and writing until now, he'd be writing to enchant the readers of today as he enchanted readers of the 1830s and 1840s.

JE: Do you do a great deal of research in the course of laying out a story? How concerned are you that the story details conform to historical fact? Would you distort history in order to tell an engaging story?

MWW: I'm a good researcher, and I do lots of it. It's painful to read something that shows a lack of research. I don't plot out short things in writing, as we used to have to do for themes in school, but any book I write has a carefully written organization, plus stacks of notes and pictures and things. If I write something historical, I do my best to recognize what happened in history. Lots of historical fiction suffers from distortion, but if this is true, it's the writer's fault. It's his responsibility to make fiction conform with fact. Too many readers are looking down your throat to see if the truth is there. You're in a mess if the truth isn't in you.

JE: You've written many stories, both in first- and third-person narratives. Do you have a specific preference?

MWW: I've written stories in the first person, notably about John and his wanderings with his guitar, but I'm not in love with the first person. All things being equal, a first-person story is like somebody telling it. A third-person story is like seeing it happen. Would you rather see a thrilling drama happen, or would you rather have somebody tell you about it? Yet, here and there, somebody can tell it in a way to share the experience with you. There are stories like that. Special stories.

JE: Are most of the names and places cited in your stories more the product of historical research or a fertile imagination?

MWW: I use real places in my stories, and, now and then, actual people. I've used, fictitiously, Charles II, John Smith, George Washington, Robert E. Lee and Ulysses S. Grant, among others, always trying to recognize the realities. I've based characters on real persons I've known, and sometimes, with permission, used real names. Imagination goes into this, of course. But, if you're trying to make a story real, where is the faint boundary between fact and fiction? Nowadays, a great deal of stuff that is offered as fact is fiction, anyway.

JE: You're particularly adept at writing dialogue. How important is it to match a character with his dialect, especially in fantasy writing?

MWW: It's important in all writing. I keep a ready ear for how people talk, because the talk proclaims the person. I deplore stilted dialogue, written out by an author for a character to read out loud, so to speak. For God's sake, let the man say what he's got to say, in his own terms. Speech must be the greatest of all inventions mankind has achieved, and certainly what you say shows what you are. Perhaps one of the greatest modern masters of dialogue was John O'Hara. If any of his characters talked in a stilted fashion, the character himself was stilted. I like the talk of real men—farmers, soldiers, hunters, workmen, sound professionals. And I don't like confected locutions, as with the far-out echelons of sociologists and advertising men and pedants generally.

JE: Do you find it difficult to think up apt titles for your stories?

MWW: Yes. I puzzle a lot over titles. Sometimes I write out several and try to choose the best. Often good titles are buried in the Bible or Bartlett's *Famous Quotations*.

JE: How interested are you in coming up with novel themes and plot ideas?

MWW: Novel themes, ideas, and treatments are hard to come by, for me anyway, and coming up with something like that gives a glorious feeling of triumph. Sometimes editors aren't as enthusiastic as I am. But when you truly get something new, and it's truly there and valid, you're like Columbus sliding in to drop another anchor off the coast of San Salvador.

JE: To what or whom do you owe your lifelong interest in mountain music, folklore, and legends?

MWW: My interest in the mountains, their music and legendry, is, I suppose, part of my lifelong interest in nature and the natural. Things are natural in those mountains. I had the great good fortune to follow two eminent folklore people around. Long ago, as an undergraduate, I was with Vance Randolph among the then unspoiled people of the Ozarks. I almost went there to live. And later, I knew and visited around in the Southern Appalachians with Bascom Lamar Lunsford. These two good men introduced me to their friends and made them friends of mine. It was a tremendously rich experience.

JE: Plant life is prominently featured in many of your stories. Kelp, pitchers, and trees come readily to mind. Does plant life hold a special fascination for you?

MWW: Yes. I'm interested in plant life of all kinds, just as I'm interested in animal life. My early boyhood years spent in West Africa may have fostered such interest. Wherever I go, I look at trees and flowers and try to identify them. I think this love of plants is one of the reasons I hate to live in big cities, where there's no nature except human nature (not always at its best). I'm fortunate to have for my brother an internationally known botanist and plant pathologist. It's a great pleasure and profit to go out among the vegetable kingdom with him. Hearing this question, I wondered, isn't everyone interested in plants? Well, maybe not everyone, except as articles of the menu.

JE: Speaking of city life, it's clear that country people loom large in your writing. Why country people? What about city folks?

MWW: I use country folks a lot in my stories because, by and large, I'm country folks myself. I live in the country and was never really at home in big cities. I've written about city people, too, and I hope believably.

JE: How much of North Carolina shows up in your work? Do you enjoy staying in your own backyard when it comes to writing?

MWW: More than half of my many books have North Carolina backgrounds or associations, and so do many of my stories. I have become a North Carolinian during my thirty-odd years of residence here, and there is much to write about in the state. I was honored with the 1978 State Award in Literature, as someone who has contributed substantially to North Carolina writing. It's a splendid state and I am proud to be identified with it.

JE: Another salient motif in your writing is Indian folklore. Are you an avid student of Indian history? What personal interest does it hold?

MWW: I've always read history with great appetite, and indeed I've written history. I don't understand those who say history doesn't interest them. Indian stories and beliefs fascinate me, and I like to hear these from Indians themselves. I'm proud of a small trickle of Indian blood in my veins.

JE: In the past, you've written convincingly about many supernatural staples—the devil, werewolves, vampires, and the like. What is the secret of treating these subjects so as to avoid becoming cliche?

MWW: The devil, werewolves, vampires, ghosts, and witches are all familiar subjects—yes, they can be called staples. As to cliches, that depends how you write about them. We're always told that there are only thirty-eight basic

13

plots in all literature, and the Greeks used them all. I never saw a list of those thirty-eight plots, by the way. However, approach is everything; otherwise there would be no point in writing anything. In your imagination there are other vampires than Dracula, other mad scientists than Frankenstein; Satan can bob up again any moment with a new, intriguing proposition to trade for your soul, and if this house is haunted, so may be the one across the street. The problem is, don't chew again exactly as somebody else has chewed.

JE: Very often you employ a format where "innocents" wander into a bizarre happening and become actively involved. Is this an important element in the fantasy genre?

MWW: Yes. The encounter of an "innocent"—usually a child—with the supernatural situation is too manifestly dramatic to need much comment. Many fine writers have used this technique, notably M. R. James, John Collier, and H. G. Wells.

JE: You are particularly deft when it comes to making frightening things one would consider powerless to frighten. For example, the imps in "For Fear of Little Men." What is the secret of this skill?

MWW: I find it hard to explain the successful effect of any of my writing. That, I suggest, is up to someone on whom the effect is successful. But the sudden frightening menace of small things is manifest. When I was in Africa, whole villages would get out of the way of a march of driver ants in their myriads; if you didn't get out of the way, they'd polish your bones. How about the Bishop of Bingen, devoured by mice? How about the excessive smallness of deadly germs? Small things can turn out horribly powerful. So much "For Fear of Little Men," and again for "Frogfather," where a cruel gigger of frogs suddenly comes face to face with a frog the size and power of an aquatic grizzly bear. I've always liked stories of the short-end coming out ahead in a fight. I remember how a big buck Belgian hare stomped to death an invading polecat. In our own chicken yard a valiant rooster, father of his country, fought and killed a chicken hawk. I heard an old hunter in the Ozarks tell of watching while a razorback boar, protecting his young piglets, fought and killed a black bear. I say don't figure the odds too confidently on such things until you see what odds pay off. There are damned unlikely victors in life.

JE: How prevalent in your work is the theme of ancient, natural forces that rise up against the presumptuous?

MWW: In what I write, there is always the situation of strange power rising up against someone who, perhaps, is over-confident. Perhaps that is influenced by the fact that I was required to read the Bible all through when I was young. You have a terrible, commanding voice of power speaking to Cain when he has killed Abel; the overwhelming of Pharaoh's chariot-borne army when the Red Sea flowed back upon it; the wiping out of the Assyrian host by a supernatural plague, in one night. Things like that have their effect on a young mind, which is instructed to believe such disasters can come to the fiercest and proudest. But you don't need the Bible to convince you of this. It's constantly true in real life. Some people call it fate. What is fate, and who operates it?

JE: In many of your stories, people pray to Satan for a variety of reasons. Does the current interest in Satanism disturb you? Are you a God-fearing man? Is religion an important personal influence?

MWW: Satanism is being practiced a lot these days, thumb-handedly. What Satan seems to stand for isn't my fancy; but he's about as fascinating a personality as ever came along. My religion is one of questioning. I suppose I'm a Christian at heart, though not an awfully good one. Satanism doesn't frighten me, though on occasion it disgusts me.

JE: Do many of your story ideas come to you through dreams, such as "The Undead Soldier?"

MWW: Maybe I haven't dreamed many whole stories, but often I wake up with something I can use in a story. It may be a strange but vivid landscape—unknown and unknowable cities show themselves in dreams, sometimes—or it may be a new character. That character may be strange to my wakeaday life, or perhaps just someone briefly encountered who, in the dream, becomes important. Dream-women occur and are worth putting into stories, especially. I'm sure that if I described some of my dreams to a psychoanalyst, he'd be like a kid in a candy store.

JE: One theme that doesn't surface too often in your writing is the idea of a life hereafter. What are your thoughts on the subject, both personally and as a story device?

MWW: I'm afraid I don't know what the life hereafter is, though I imagine there is such a thing. I haven't written much about it, except when I use a ghost in a story.

JE: Do you write with the idea of conveying a specific message to the reader?

MWW: No. I've never thought of writing for "message," which suggests advertising copy. If I have a message, perhaps it is that life is interesting.

JE: How do you perceive your role as a writer? Do you primarily write to entertain or do you also have certain didactic goals?

MWW: This is a tricky two-choice question. Entertainer? If I were going to be that, I'd have done better in show business. I was an actor once; if I'd stayed with it, I could play Falstaff or Big Daddy now. However, the other side of the question is: Am I going to be didactic, preach a sermon? I never truly wanted to be an actor or a preacher. I hope the point, or the lesson, isn't that simple. I start out by trying to be happy (though frantically busy) with what I write. Sometimes readers have been diverted, entertained to read it. Once or twice or more times than that, readers have confessed that they learned and were inspired. I suppose that the entertainer can inspire and teach now and then. Likewise, the preacher might amuse, as with Billy Sunday or Amy Semple McPherson. But here you've given me two extremes, and there's a little room between and on both sides.

JE: When writing a book, what kind of reader or audience do you have in mind? Does this assessment shape the scope and direction of your work?

MWW: Except for the juveniles I've written, slanted at young readers, I think simply of writing for literate human beings. I've been gratified to find that I'm read and relished by readers of all sorts, ages, and backgrounds.

JE: From your vantage point, what makes for a successful fantasy story? What ingredients must it possess?

MWW: A fantasy tale should take the extraordinary situation, make it real, and make the reader believe it and accept it. Farnsworth Wright's favorite word was "convincing." I used to get tired of it, but I know how right he was to insist.

JE: What does it take to be a successful fantasy writer? Is a particular attitude required?

MWW: A fantasy writer needs the sense of wonder in a high degree. I can't speak to "attitude"—good writers of fantasy vary from happy souls like Seabury Quinn to bizarre, mixed-up tragic ones like Robert E. Howard.

JE: What other advice would you give to aspiring young fantasy writers? How should they approach the genre? Should they search for new themes?

MWW: Study the field; write the best you possibly can; study markets and try to suit them. And don't wait for the "mood" to strike; you may go hungry before it shows up. Writing is more than a profession, it's a priesthood. approach it as such. As to areas heretofore untapped, try to find one, or more than one.

JE: Do you view fantasy, especially as you write it, as "escapist" in nature? Is escapism a good thing?

MWW: Fantasy is "escapist" literature, which, by the way, is badly needed these sordid days. Escapist literature is somewhat akin to dreams. If you dream a dream with a happy ending, you wake up and are happy to have dreamed it If it's a horrible dream, you wake up and are glad you're awake. Escapism is sometimes used as a derogatory term. But I feel it's like falling into a cesspool. You're supposed to stay in there and brilliantly adjust to your environment. But if you scramble out and have a bath, you're an escapist. I wonder how people in hell feel on this subject?

JE: Like many fantasy writers, a number of your stories contain elements of violence and mayhem. Is this an integral component of the fantasy genre? Have you ever been critized for excessive blood and gore?

MWW: I hadn't thought my stories were full of these things. Now and then, old ladies of both sexes complain about violence in there, but I've tried to be restrained in that as in all else. Violence, alas, is an active principle of the human mind and soul.

JE: As you see it, what is the best means of ensuring the believability of a fantasy story?

MWW: To make your story believable, get to believing it yourself. Thomas Wolfe said that, or something like that, in *The Web and the Rock*. For the time when you're writing, those people must be more real than the flesh-and-blood people who just might drop in and interrupt you. You must see every blade of grass, every rock and bush. If you have something uncanny, you must make it uncanny, don't just say it's uncanny. This—the presentation of the monster or specter—is hardest of all. M. R. James could do it. So, sometimes, could Algernon Blackwood, Lord Dunsany, and James Branch Cabell. I repeat, it's hard, and you'd better think and think and revise and revise. And read how others brought it off, but don't copy them.

JE: How has fantasy, as a literature, changed since you first started writing?

MWW: Naturally, the ways of fantasy have changed, but fantasy traditions are solid. Perhaps this can be attributed to the fact that so much of fantasy refers to old beliefs and reports, dating back to the beginning of communicated folklore. Of course, we learn to write in new ways. Published stories these days are, or should be, written in language that today's readers can understand and appreciate. Yet it is significant that people still read and like things written by old writers now long dead, who should be alive today to enjoy their success. This sustained popularity is one of the acid tests of good writing.

JE: Does writing come easier to you today than when you began your career?

MWW: I hope I write better now than when I was young, but no, by God, I don't write easier than I did then. Maybe I have more of a writer's way of life; but if I wrote easily, I'd be suspicious of my own writing.

JE: Are there any fantasy writers who you wish you were more like, either in terms of richness of ideas or facility with language?

MWW: I admire many writers, particularly the English ones. What I may most admire is style and perception. I should say here that the writers I most admire aren't necessarily in the fantasy field. Let's say Shakespeare, Dante, and Milton; Russians, like Tolstoy and Dostoyevsky; the French, like Flaubert, Maupassant, and Stendhal; the English, like Thackeray, Dickens, and more modern writers, like Hardy, Kipling, Conrad (though he was a Pole writing in England) and, later, Wodehouse, Waugh, and so on; Americans, like Twain, Whitman, London, Fitzgerald, Faulkner, Hemingway, and Wolfe. I admire all these great gifts in richness of invention and the language in which to express it. But I can't let myself envy. Envy is a small, despicable impulse. I've been influenced, yes, but I work hard at being my own sort of man and writer. I don't want to imitate.

JE: Unlike many modern fantasy writers, you were quite shy and withdrawn when it came to self-promotion. Why?

MWW: When I was young, I was taught that self-promotion—beating drums and waving flags for your own publicity—was in bad taste. I accepted that viewpoint while I was rebelling against others, and I still think it's a good viewpoint. When people interview me and ask me questions, I do my best to be agreeable and helpful, but I hate to seek such things out. I know writers who do go in for melodramatic self-advertisement, and I feel embarrassed for them. I wish they didn't think they needed it. I'm grateful to those who know me best, who mostly seem to approve of me as a human being. And I'm grateful to those who don't know me personally at all, but like what I write.

JE: Have you, the artist, and you, the commercial writer, been able to work well together over the years?

MWW: It's for others to evalute me as an artist. As a commercial writer, I don't think I've tried to be that. Some people can do that brilliantly, but I don't think I know how. I'm afraid that I've thought more about trying to write the best I knew how. Maybe that got me some rejects years ago, though the rejects have been polished and sold later. I'd like to think that, in the last ditch, the editor can't reject you if only you've written well enough to break his legs and make him accept you. Of course, you must recognize the facts of writing life and try to cope with them outside any ivory towers. But I'm no great success at commercialism, or I'd have been the greatest advertising copy writer in the world.

JE: As you look back over your career, do you have any deep regrets, things that you would do differently if you had the opportunity?

MWW: Mostly, if I had it all to do over again, I'd have stuck more faithfully to what most moved me to write, would have tried to spend less time in writing, as I had to, to get eating money. It would have been good to have been born a little later, to be still young in these times when the fantasy genre is so well accepted. As it is, I hope I have more or less succeeded with what I felt I must do. And who knows what I might have done with another life? The whole life-long experience has been intensely valuable to me, not only as a writer but as a man. Every single damned aspect of it. If I'd done things differently, undoubtedly, I'd have been somebody else than who I am.

JE: Looking back, what accounts for your extraordinary staying power as a writer?

MWW: I've written for half a century because I love to write and developed an early interest in it as a career. I wouldn't be happy if I weren't writing. I'd write if I had a million dollars a year, tax free. I've been lucky in having extremely good health and good opportunities to get published, as well as a sustained and sustaining interest in life and in finding out new things all the time. Yet it will be too bad if I don't know when I'm through and can't write any more. Nothing is so pathetic as somebody who didn't hear the whistle and realize the game was over, so far as he was concerned.

JE: If you were asked to assess your work, how would you do so? What are your primary strengths and limitations?

MWW: They say that one who acts as his own lawyer has a fool for a client. It may be suggested that one who assesses his own work has a fool for a critic. So I walk delicately here. I can only hope that I have done honest work in the best way I can, and that it reads honestly and well. Maybe I've done something good with solid folk themes, complete with natural people as they act and speak and think. I've done my best to stay away from pumped-up, hyperbolic writing. My chief limitation, today as when I began, is in not writing as well as I wish I could.

JE: How do you view your own contribution to the fantasy field? How would you like to be remembered?

MWW: If I've made an appreciable contribution, I hope it was for honesty and for writing my best. I've been flattered by the expressed opinions of folk-lorists that I have some value as an interpreter of the natural American and things he may believe. And I've tried to write with decent restraint, too, tried to do it without capital letters and exclamation points. One thing else I seem to have done, if I am to judge by what is said and written about me, is the capture and recording in my stories of old folk songs. I wish I could do more in that area.

JE: Do you still read much fantasy? How would you assess the current crop of new writers? Who are your favorites in the field today?

MWW: I read fantasy all the time, the old and the new. Among my favorites are many personal friends. Robert Bloch comes forcibly to mind. Of the British writers, I see Ramsey Campbell as coming strongly to the fore. Here in America, I think Karl Edward Wagner has taken the place Robert E. Howard had long ago. I can't name everyone.

JE: Finally, what do you most enjoy doing when you're not writing? What do you do in your spare time?

MWW: At present I am well up in years, and don't do some things I used to do. When I was young I loved rough sports. I played football, I was thought to be a good boxer and fencer, and I hiked long distances, climbed mountains, camped out, watched animals, and studied plants and minerals. These days, I only watch sports. I travel when I can, and when I travel I'm always happy to make friends with good strangers. I'm a pretty sociable person. I like to go to parties with the right sort (especially writers to talk shop). I greatly enjoy good food and drink (my wife, who also writes, is way up there among the best cooks I've ever known). I like to listen to music—all kinds—from high-flown classical to earthy, traditional folk. And when I have time I read and read. All these things, I hope, make me a good representative specimen of the human race.

JOHN NORMAN: THE CHRONICLES OF GOR

Who is "John Norman?" This question has baffled readers and critics alike for years. Indeed, rumors of all kinds have circulated as to the well-guarded identity of one of the world's most successful (as measured by total book sales) science fiction-fantasy writers. Now, in this exclusive interview, Dr. John Lange, aka "John Norman," answers many of the questions which have sparked this debate, questions relating not only to the author's identity, but to his controversial "Gorean" series. For the first time in print, speaking first-hand, Lange talks about himself and his work, in what amounts to one of the liveliest and most provocative interviews of its kind ever published.

Having disclosed Norman's identity, the next appropriate question is: who is "John Lange?" The answer to this question was extremely difficult to come by, as there is virtually no authoritative public information available about the author. Indeed, this interviewer unsuccessfully combed nearly fifty reference works in search of such information. Although Lange was quite willing to discuss the topic of this interview, he was much more reticent to divulge information about himself and his background. However, after several follow-up letters, the author supplied the following personal data.

John Lange was born in Chicago, Illinois, on June 3, 1931. He is married and has three children, two boys and one girl. Lange is a professor of philosophy at Queens College of the City University of New York, in Flushing, New York, where he specializes in the areas of epistemology, logic, and innovational conceptualization. The author received a B.A. from the University of Nebraska, an M.A. from the University of Southern California, and a Ph.D. from Princeton University. Lange has published several scholarly works, including *The Cognitivity Paradox: An Inquiry Concerning the Claims of Philosophy* and *Values and Imperatives: Studies in Ethics,* which he edited.

The author has worked, at one time or another, either part-time or full-time, as a radio announcer and writer for KOLN, Lincoln, Nebraska; a film writer for the University of Nebraska; and a story analyst for Warner Brothers Motion Pictures, Inc., in Burbank, California. He has also worked as a technical editor and special materials writer for Rocketdyne, a Division of North American Aviation, Inc., specializing in the production of rocket engines.

Lange's first professional sale was a radio script to a station in Lincoln, Nebraska, when he was in high school, or somewhere thereabouts. Under the pseudonym, "John Norman," he has published a number of popular works, among which are the "Gorean" books. Lange is a member of the Science Fiction Writers of America and the American Philosophical Association.

JE: Can you say how you started as a science fiction-fantasy writer?

JN: Yes. I think this probably has something to do with one's imagination and its nature. Certain sorts of imaginations probably lend themselves more readily to different literary genres. As a modality of self-expression, adventure fantasy seems attractive, rich, and natural to me. I'm sorry this is not a better answer. Why do some people paint, others compose music? And if one paints, why do some paint landscapes and others . . .? I do not think I will attempt to respond further to this question.

JE: What is it about the genre, if anything, that accounts for your interest?

JN: Let us suppose that a lion hunts antelopes. Does he hunt antelopes because there is something about antelopes that accounts for his interest? That sounds like a very rational decision process was involved. He probably hunts antelopes because he is a lion, and, being a lion, antelopes look good to him. Similarly, I suspect that I write adventure fantasy because I have a certain sort of imagination. Because of the way I am, perhaps, it looks good to me.

JE: Why did you choose to write under a pseudonym as opposed to your actual name?

JN: I have a family to support. At the time the first Gorean book was published, I did not have tenure at my academic institution. I did not wish to be denied tenure, and be out of a job, with no explanations given, but the reason being, perhaps, that I had dared to do something so academically disreputable as write science fiction. This situation has been ameliorated somewhat in the

19

academic world in the last few years, but I think it is still true to say that, for the most part, it is academically customary to belittle and dismiss science fiction. For example, I think a young man or woman in an English department would do well, even today, to keep a low profile about an interest in science fiction, if he or she is interested in tenure, promotion, etc. To my mind, there remains today in the academic world a great deal of prejudice against the genre. For example, at my own institution, science fiction, for purposes of fellowship-leave applications, does not count as "creative" work. That is interesting, I think, for science fiction and adventure fantasy are probably the most creative of the literary genres. If it had not been for the tenure problem, I do not think I would have used a pseudonym. On the other hand, I think "John Norman" is an excellent writing name, and I am pleased with it. My own name, John Lange, incidentally, is almost never pronounced correctly. That would seem a count against it, at least as a writing name. Furthermore, it, hilariously, is used by at least one other writer as his *pseudonym.*

JE: To what extent is John Lange knowable through his fiction? In what sense can your work be described as autobiographical?

JN: I do not think I am qualified to respond to this question. It is very difficult to know oneself, let alone worry about how aspects of one's personality might be expressed in one's work. Obviously, something of oneself must be involved in all honest creative work. On the other hand, I doubt that psychology is yet ready to make serious judgments on such matters. There are just too many unknowns in the equation, and it is difficult to control and correlate the writer variables, the analyzer variables, and the work variables. To be sure, anyone who has read the Gorean books surely knows me better than if he had not read them. On the other hand, it is necessary to read the books intelligently and honestly. If the books are read unintelligently and hysterically, the result, I think, would be that the reader would finish up knowing very little about either the books or me.

JE: Unlike most writers, you have studiously avoided publicity. Why?

JN: I have not, perhaps, as studiously avoided publicity as many people think. I have, for example, publicly addressed various science-fiction conventions and various science-fiction groups. On the other hand, I think it is quite true that I have not made a practice of actively seeking publicity. First, it is not my nature to do so. Second, as is no secret, various individuals in the science-fiction community bear me great hostility. This is obvious in emotive, abusive, slanderous reviews. Accordingly, I see no point in entering more actively into the affairs of the science-fiction community. It is natural, incidentally, for these individuals to wish to control and limit science fiction. That I outsell them, say, forty or fifty to one, also, has perhaps contributed to their pique. Some of these individuals take themselves very seriously, in spite of their having no obvious justification in doing so. Some resent my extending the perimeters of science fiction into new areas, this perhaps seeming to reflect adversely on their own work, which might then, in contrast, appear unprogressive, sterile, and juvenile. It is popular to call for "new directions" in science fiction, but when one shows up, it seems that panic sets in. "New directions" usually means new wrinkles or variations on old variations or old themes, within the limitations of certain orthodox structures. They are thrilled by new hardware, which is safe; they are terrified by an attempt to treat human beings honestly, rather than as Victorian abstractions. I do not bear these people ill will. They are doubtless as innocent as mice and rabbits. On the other hand, I think one of the reasons for the isolation of John Norman in the science-fiction community, in spite of the fact that he is, I gather, the best-selling, or one of the best-selling authors in the genre, is to be explained in virtue of the hatred of a few individuals who wish to control, limit, and direct the destiny of science fiction and, too, of course, for the future of up-and-coming writers who are not willing to spend years brown-nosing their way into the club. One may then similarly hope that many other new writers may, in their own chosen ventures, be fortunate enough to speak the truth as they see it. Not only are the old lies repetitious, they do not even sell very well. It is the readers, in the final analysis, who have made John Norman successful. It is the readers, in the final analysis, who have made John Norman successful. In spite of what might happen in the future, for example, that certain individuals might eventually become successful in managing to fully implement the censorship implicit in the position, it will always be the case that, at least for a few years, something was done against them and beyond them which was itself, and was, in its way, whether correct or incorrect, proud and magnificent. The Gorean books exist.

JE: How would you characterize the kind of writing you do? Is it fair to label it "sword and sorcery" in content?

JN: I dislike labels and categories. They can be useful, but often they become stereotypes, and one then tends to view matters not as they are, in their own fullness and uniqueness, but under the attributes of stereotypes. This is a cruel error where human beings are concerned and, logically, it does not improve in validity when the move is made to artifacts, musical compositions, stories, etc. The genre I write is, so to speak, "the Gorean novels." They are, for most practical purposes, their own genre. If one had to use labels, I would think that something like "adventure fantasy" would be rather good. They are certainly *not* "sword and sorcery." For example, magic is not involved in the books. Similarly, great attention is given to scientific versimilitude, within, of course, artistic latitude. The Gorean books, incidentally, are one of the few productions in science fiction which take seriously things like human biology and depth psychology. I'm not announcing anything new if I point out that there is very little science, normally, science fiction. Indeed, if one were merely interested in coming up with category titles which were more descriptive than "science fiction" of what actually goes on in "science fiction," presumably one would speak of something like "engineering fiction" or "technology fiction." Furthermore, what science, as opposed to applied science (e.g., space ships), occurs in science fiction is usually limited to the physical sciences, or, in more knowledgeable writers, the social sciences. The human sciences (i.e., human biology and psychology) are usually avoided, perhaps because they involve areas "too close to home."

JE: Do you have specific requirements when it comes to writing "adventure fantasy?"

JN: I once knew a musician who would ask himself the following critical question about his music: "Does it sound?" Not being a musician, I am not fully cognizant of what he may have had in mind, but, clearly, he was not asking if it was audible or not. I think he was suggesting that there was a "rightness" about it which might be difficult or impossible to analyze, but which, if attained, would be recognizable. His test of good music then was "whether or not it sounded." It is hard to teach music on this kind of premise, but perhaps there is no other test or touchstone for excellence in that genre. Similarly, in writing, I suspect that all, or most, authors use a similar sort of subjective yet essential and significant test. "Does it sound?" Is it terrific? Is it marvelous? Does it make you want to leap out of your chair and scream for joy? More simply, is

21

it good? Is it right? In this sense, I would like for my work to be "good," to be "right," indeed, to be "great." Greatness is my objective. I would rather fail to have grasped a star than never to have lifted my head to the sky.

JE: Are you a meticulous writer? Do you labor over your work? Do you do much rewriting?

JN: Interestingly, the Gorean books write themselves. I do not know if other authors have this experience or not. I hope so, for it saves a great deal of work. The Gorean books are not put together like shelves, according to outlines or plans drawn up beforehand. They are more in the nature of organic products which grow. They are more like flowers and trees than reports and machines. I know when a book is ready. Then I sit down and watch it unfold. I am sometimes an amazed, delighted spectator. It is like something going on over which I have very little control. It is more like a welcome gift. Why should I ask questions? If the book is not "there," then I do not know if it could be written or not. I have never hacked a book. When a book is ready, I have humbly accepted it, gratefully. On the hypothesis that these books are not dictated through me by some foreign intelligence, which would seem pretty screwy, I must suspect that they are extremely deeply related to subconscious creative processes. I am pretty much, perhaps unfortunately, at the mercy of such processes. As the Eskimos say, "No one knows from where songs come." I do, of course, before turning in a manuscript, do some revising and some rewriting. I can sweat blood over commas, like any beleaguered writer. On the other hand, if my information is correct, I probably expend fewer dues for literary torture than many authors. I hope so, for it sounds as though some of those fellows really suffer. I have nothing against suffering, incidentally. I just don't care to do it myself.

JE: Given the nature of your work, do you feel any special obligation to your readers? If so, what?

JN: I have general obligations to human beings, and I have obligations to myself. I have special obligations to my family, etc. I am not clearly aware that I have special obligations to my readers, beyond those which I would have towards other human beings. I hope, of course, that they will enjoy my work. I do not think I have an obligation to please my readers, for example, but I would naturally hope that I would. In the final analysis, I write for myself. I wish to please mostly myself. If an artist cannot be true to himself, how can he be true to anyone else? I think my readers expect me to be honest with myself. My first obligation is thus to truth and integrity. If I can fulfill this obligation, I think then that my readers, or more of them, will be satisfied.

JE: How do you view your role as a writer—entertainer, observer, reformer?

JN: I do not think of writing as a "role." Similarly, I do not think of eating and sleeping as roles. Writing is something which, for me, is very natural. Accordingly, it is difficult for me to try and answer this question. I write primarily for myself. I wish to please myself. I wish to come up with something great. Therefore, I do not primarily consider myself in "other-related" roles (e.g., entertainer, observer, reformer). One must beware of defining oneself in relation to others. I am myself. So are most other people, if they only knew it.

JE: How much would you admit to modelling your characters on real people?

JN: This seems an oddly-phrased question. There is a sense in which I suppose most literary characters are modelled on "real" people. This seems something less to be "admitted" than something which it would be difficult to doubt. To be sure, characters, if interesting and believable, must have "real" characteristics, the characteristics of "real" people. One of the problems with much science fiction is that the background, perhaps because of its exotic nature, tends to intrude too much into the story and often distracts from elements such as plot and characterization. I think that characterization, in particular, is difficult for many writers in science fiction because of the unusual "scenery" involved. It is hard to get involved with a particular character when unusual appliances and gadgets are clicking and blinking, and whistling and zooming in the vicinity. This is an advantage that more pedestrian genres usually have over science fiction; that the background, because of its prosaic nature, can commonly be taken for granted, and the author can concentrate on character development and conflict. One of the strengths of Robert Heinlein, I think, is his capacity to handle characterization. Aside from his own considerable talent, one of his devices in this matter, it seems to me, is not to bite off more than he can chew in the matter of a specific background at a specific time. The background in Heinlein commonly gives us an enhancing setting for human concerns. In Heinlein, people are *there*, really. In certain other authors, things seem to take precedence over people; such authors are perhaps less interested in people than in things. From my own point of view, I find both interesting. People, however, I must admit, come first. Incidentally, in the case of the Gorean books, the backgrounds are usually simple enough, and familiar enough, from the past history of Earth, and easily understandable extrapolations of barbaric cultures, to be fairly unobtrusive. Gorean backgrounds, thus, seldom distract from the interpersonal relations involved. Indeed, a great deal of attention is often given, in Gorean novels, to interpersonal relations, sometimes of a dramatic and interesting nature. Similarly, character development is extremely important. Most characters in science fiction, as you know, begin as, and remain substantially, the cardboard stereotypes of juvenile hero literature. Indeed, one of the difficulties which some people have with the Gorean books is that their familiar and predictable stereotypes do not occur. The Gorean books present an *ethos* which is not that of most Earthlings, and indeed, for which a great deal is to be said. The Gorean books suggest that human beings dare to think truly alternative realities, not just the old realities projected into an exotic environment. Perhaps the fear to do this motivates some of the abusive and hysterical reactions which the Gorean books have aroused. It seems tragic when individuals who are supposedly original and daring thinkers, by profession even, are suddenly revealed, in basic matters, to be truly afraid of thinking. Or, perhaps, it is all right to think about machines; it is only ourselves, perhaps, about which we must not dare to think. Thought, of course, is dangerous. It is the instrument of change.

JE: What degree of reality do your characters have for you once you've finished writing about them?

JN: This seems something of an odd question, too. The characters in the Gorean novels, for what it is worth, seem extremely real to me. I am confident that I know how they feel about things, where their "heads are at," and how they would be likely to respond in given instances. I suspect any author feels this way about characters. If the character is not real, it seems it would be difficult to write about him, or her, or it. Surely, the reality of such a character does not cease when one ceases writing about him.

JE: Do you write with a specific audience in mind? Do you tailor your work for this audience?

JN: Perhaps I write because I have to. If that is the case, then questions about particular audiences become somewhat irrelevant. I do, of course, wish to please myself. Perhaps that is relevant. This might be a good point to mention a theory I have about literary selection. The analogy, of course, is to natural selection. Let us suppose an animal is born with a certain set of physical properties and behavioral dispositions. Obviously, these properties and dispositions will influence its survival in a given environment. For example, in some environments, thick fur and certain serum may be of value, and in other environments thin fur and different serum factors. Genetics, so to speak, throws the dice and the environment selects the winning numbers. A similar phenomenon occurs in evolving social and technological environments. Hero of Alexandria, in the second century B.C., constructs a novel toy; James Watt, in the eighteenth century A.D., building on the work of earlier inventors, designs an improved steam engine, and alters the nature and direction of human civilizations. I think a similar phenomenon has occurred with the Gorean books. I have done what is right and natural and honest, at least from my point of view. I have not attempted to please critics or conform to a market. I have been myself. I think this comes through in my writing. I am self-directed, rather than other-directed. I have kept my integrity. It has been my good fortune that the Gorean books are apparently needed in our contemporary civilization. Obviously, they answer to certain deep needs in human beings. If they were not important to people, and if they did not have something important to say, something which apparently desperately needs saying, they would not be as popular as they are.

JE: How would you describe your audience? Who buys a John Norman novel?

JN: It is difficult to answer this question without market research. Fan mail, of course, and sales in special outlets, such as college bookstores, provide us with some evidence. My impression is that the Gorean books are read and enjoyed by individuals of all ages and backgrounds. The sales, for example, for better or worse, indicate that the audience for them extends far beyond the borders of the science-fiction community. They have been on best-seller lists many times, for example. Unlike the usual science-fiction sales of a few thousand books, if one is lucky, they have sold millions of copies. Gorean books, too, incidentally, if it is of any interest, have been published in several languages. Certainly, many women are avid fans of the Gorean series. Indeed, I think one of the contributions, not likely to be acknowledged, which the Gorean books have made commercially to the science-fiction field is that they have helped open it up to female interest. In this sense, I think I have brought or have probably brought, many new readers to science fiction, not only male, but also female. The success of the Gorean books, I think, tends to improve the sales of other science-fiction books, or adventure-fantasy books, by encouraging interest in the genre and enlarging the market. I, personally, am very fond of my audience. Their encouragement and support is deeply appreciated.

JE: Would you enjoy reading your own books, had you not written them? Do you read other authors who write in a similar vein?

JN: This is a hard question to answer, because I *have* written the books. It is thus hard to look at them objectively, as though, say, they might have been written by someone else. Since I think the books are marvelous and interesting, etc., I certainly hope that I would enjoy reading them. On the other hand, I can conceive of feeling extreme frustration, anger, and disappointment if I read them, and had not written them, for then I think I would have wished that it had been I, and not the other fellow, who had written them. Perhaps I would be angry that he had "gotten there first." I do not read other authors who write in the same vein. I might if there were any. I don't know. John Norman, at least at the moment, for better or for worse, is the only fellow in his field. My field, of course, is my sort of novel, that sort of novel which I have pioneered.

24

I am tolerant of diversity in the science-fiction field, incidentally. I do not have a set of *a priori* notions as to what counts as science fiction or not; I do not limit myself to certain traditional paradigms of propriety. I encourage each author to be true and honest to himself. The major danger which science fiction faces is self-imposed limitations, probably largely functions of psychological and cultural blocks.

JE: How much research, planning, and study do you do before actually writing a novel?

JN: As with most authors, my work is a result, at least in part, of resources accumulated over many years. As a youngster in high school, for example, I had an interest in ancient history. The first serious book I ever read, as I recall, was the *Meditations of Marcus Aurelius*. I remember reading it at the wrestling matches. Upon occasion, of course, specific research is in order for a given book; for example, in connection with one project or another, I have investigated, or deepened my investigations, of such matters as Roman naval construction, Medieval shipping, Viking sports, the economics of oases, Eskimo weaponry, and the flora and fauna of rain forests. I usually limit specific research to a dozen or so and a few days' time. After all, I am not writing, say, a novel of Napoleonic France, which would require incredible fidelity to historical details. I am writing adventure fantasy. The Gorean world, of course, has been heavily influenced by our world; on the other hand, it is *not* our world. Thus, there must be a creative contribution to the construction of the world. In that sense, in adventure fantasy, research must serve a purpose beyond familiarizing oneself with certain facts; one must not content oneself merely with the replication of past realities. Instead, one must consider how such things, in a different situation in time, might become altered or transformed. Indeed, perhaps new inventions and cultural practices, etc., would be developed. The major value of research, I think, in this sort of situation, is not to limit, but rather to stimulate and enrich, the creative purpose. Aside from questions of research, I do not do much actual planning of my books. For example, as explained earlier, I prefer to let the book happen by itself, while I watch it. I am around, so to speak, while it is being written. I do, of course, generally have a background in mind, and sometimes a general problem or line of development. How can one make a map of territories he has never seen? How can he chart lands which he has not yet explored?

JE: What are the salient themes or problems which typify a Gorean novel?

JN: This is an interesting question. Many themes occur and reoccur in the Gorean books. One of the major themes, of course, is the complex interplay between social and biological elements; another theme is the attempt to inquire into the nature of human beings; still, others are, friendship, courage, and love.

JE: Do you think highly of your own work? Do your books give you much pride?

JN: Yes. I think highly of my own work. It is the finest thing, of its sort, ever to be done in adventure fantasy. Whether or not one should be proud of one's work, on the other hand, is a more complex and interesting question. The moral question here, for a humanist and a naturalist, is a knotty one. It is particularly acute in my case because the books, as I have mentioned, pretty much write themselves. I do not know if I should take credit, in that sense, for them or not. I welcome them as gifts. I do not know if I am "proud" that songs come to me. I am, of course, undeniably grateful.

JE: Do you have a favorite among your books? If so, what? Which is your least favorite, and why?

JN: I do not think it is wise on an author's part to respond to this sort of inquiry. One loves all one's children.

JE: What is it about your novels that explains their widespread popularity?

JN: I don't know. Hopefully, they are well written and exciting. Perhaps the readers find the Gorean world of interest. Perhaps the books touch on neglected or suppressed human constants, male and female. Perhaps they have something to say which has not been said for a long time. They are probably unique, or almost so, in modern literature, in raising serious questions about the intellectual superstructure of western civilization. They have intellectual content. There are ideas in them. Perhaps that is what so outrages some critics. Science fiction, however, or at least from my point of view, can be a literature with cognitive content. No one would deny that in principle, yet how few have troubled themselves to put it into practice. To paraphrase Nietzshe, the problem is not to have the courage of one's convictions; that is easy. The problem is to have the courage for an attack on one's convictions.

JE: Do you care what the critics think about your work?

JN: No.

JE: Have you found that the critics tend to understand your objectives?

JN: I read very little criticism. Accordingly, I do not know whether critics, on the whole, understand my objectives or not. Indeed, I am not sure that I understand my own objectives, or even if I have "objectives" in the sense suggested by the question. If that is the case, I guess the critics must indeed have a hard time with my work. As mentioned earlier, the books pretty much write themselves. If that is the case, I'm not sure that talk of "objectives" is all that relevant to them. Perhaps a plan has an objective, or a baseball, but I'm not sure that a novel does. Does a mountain or a tree have an objective? I do, of course, wish to write great books. Perhaps that is an objective. That would seem to be a simple enough objective. Perhaps a critic could understand that. I would hope so.

JE: Does writing serve a cathartic function for you? Does it teach you important things about yourself and what you value?

JN: I enjoy writing, and I'm happy when I do it. Perhaps some sort of cathartic value is involved. I do not know. I suppose it would be. I just don't know. There are probably many values, of a diverse nature, connected with writing. I would also suppose that one knows more about oneself when one has written a book than before. Similarly, when one has written a book, I suppose one might be clearer about either what one has valued or what one has decided to value than one might have been before.

JE: How important is artistic excellence when it comes to your writing? Do you aspire to a certain artistic standard?

JN: I am not the sort of fellow who presents himself either as an "artist" or a "craftsman." These seem to me vanity costumes. I am less concerned with being an artist or a craftsman than I am with writing the book. My focus is on the work, not myself. It has been my experience that those fellows who make a great deal out of themselves as being "artists" or "only humble craftsmen," etc., are less likely to be either good artists or craftsmen than the fellows who forget about that role garbage and are work-oriented, not image-oriented. The real artist, or craftsman, is hard to find on the cocktail circuit; he is too busy in the studio trying to get some effect or another right. Does that sprinkling can belong in the picture or not? He may paint it in and out a dozen times. He is not worrying about his image; he is worrying about the sprinkling can.

JE: How do you respond to the charge that your books exploit sex and violence—that they debase and debauch the human spirit?

JN: There seem to me two very different charges here. Let's consider them separately. First, the word "exploit" is, of course, a hostile word, a signal word, chosen, I assume deliberately, to prejudice a reader. It is not the sort of expression an objective individual would choose. On the other hand, let us not quibble about semantics. Certainly, sex and violence occur in the Gorean novels. They are significant plot elements. Perhaps to the horror of the critic, I see no reason to be apologetic about this. I guess I am just less guilty or timid, or something, than he is. Though the critic will not understand this, judging by the intellectual or emotional level suggested in the criticism, sex and violence are both real parts of life. History and human reality would be inexplicable without them. They belong in any strong, honest literature. To advocate writing an emotionally truncated, expurgated, namby-pamby literature is, I suppose, permissible, but, it seems to me, it is certainly not desirable. Indeed, from my own point of view, such a refusal to write honestly constitutes a betrayal of literature which I find not only aesthetically offensive but unreasonable and, I think, morally improper. The question here is a simple one: Is the writer to be honest to life, in its fullness, or not? I would think so, but that is my own answer. I cannot answer for others. Let those who fear to think and feel write without emotion and thought. Incidentally, while we are on the topic, it might also be noted, in fairness, that the Gorean books exploit discipline, courage, nobility, honor, and love. The human being, with his heights and glories, his depths and cruelties, exceeded in complexity and reality the abstractions and idealizations of the frightened and the weak. It will always be thus. I love man and fear him; thus I will celebrate him. I will try to honor him as being as he is, not as fools might wish him. The second charge has something to do with "debasing and debauching the human spirit." It is difficult to know how to respond to a criticism of this sort, because it is difficult to know if the critic intends it to be understood literally or figuratively. If the critic intends it to be taken literally, it seems to be obviously false. There is no such thing, literally, as far as I can tell, as "the human spirit." Accordingly, it can neither be debased nor debauched. Similarly, there is no such thing, strictly, as far as I can tell, as a "giraffe spirit" or the "spirit of apple pie." On the other hand, on the assumption that the critic is at least vaguely aware of developments in science in the past 120 years, in particular in the sciences of biology, psychology and anthropology, we may assume that he intended it figuratively. But if this is so, it might mean a number of different things. Accordingly, he could always claim that whichever possibility I chose to discuss was not that which he intended. On the other hand, since that cannot be helped and is a predictable response, I think I have little choice but to steam ahead. Accordingly, I shall do so. The "human spirit," I am afraid, for better or for worse, is more complicated than our critic understands. All things that human beings do are manifestations of the "human spirit." If the critic would understand the nature of the "human spirit," I suggest to him that he consult the tapestries and pageants of history. In those bloody threads he will find its biography delineated. There he will discover that hunting, and pride, and lust and victory, are as much authentic manifestations of the "human spirit" as the planting of flowers and the dreams of innocence. Indeed, they seem more germane to its iron and its songs than hypocrisy and lace. One of the strengths of the Gorean books, in my opinion, is that they constitute one of the few places in contemporary literature where the "human spirit," as it exists in reality, and not in the abstractions of political mythologies, is neither denied nor distorted. The Gorean books celebrate the "human spirit" in its fullness, in its darkness and its glory, in its pettiness and cruelty, in its shame and in its incomparable splendors.

JE: Are you surprised by the tremendous controversy that surrounds your work? Why do you think such controversy exists?

JN: Yes, I'm surprised. I'm not sure why there is so much controversy. The books seem to be pretty innocent. After all, what is so terrible about taking ethnology or depth psychology seriously? I think the reasons for the controversy are irrational, rather than rational. Apparently, some people read the Gorean books with the dispassionate objectivity of a psychotic interpreting Rorschach blots. They see anything they wish to see in them. As a result of these projections, they are apparently sometimes disturbed. One has trouble, for example, with the sexual hysterics. Some of these have perhaps found a refuge in science fiction, which, commonly, even today, tends to avoid coming to grips with the nature and problems of human sexuality. There are, however, doubtless many other reasons for controversy as well. Three other factors come immediately to mind. First, the resentment of certain in-group individuals to the success of a newcomer; this resentment can be rationalized, of course, in a variety of ways; one hates first, then one thinks up reasons. Second, the Gorean books present a different *ethos* and take it seriously. This frightens some people because it makes them feel insecure; everyone is supposed to have the right opinions and values—theirs. When they meet someone who presents a genuinely alternative conceptualization of reality, an intellectual alternative rather than a merely mechanical alternative, they become alarmed; they feel threatened. They are only verbally in favor of diversity of thought; their rhetoric of freedom is revealed as hypocrisy; it is belied by their bigotry and intolerance. Third, the Gorean books have introduced new subject matter and new ideas to science fiction. They have plowed new conceptual furrows; they have altered, in the thinking of thousands, the conceptions and horizons of science fiction. The borders of science fiction have been extended by my work; new possibilities have been delineated and explored. It is natural that these changes would be felt as threatening to a vain, stale, insecure establishment. Will the old formulas no longer work? Will their own work seem unimaginative and juvenile by contrast? Will they suffer a loss in prestige? Are the Huns truly at the gates? If I knew how, I would like to reassure these frightened people. They have their strengths and weaknesses, as I do; they have their naiveties, their stupidities, their frailties, as I do. Perhaps the Hun at the gates is not really so different from themselves as they might fear. Perhaps he, too, has a respect and affection for the genre. Science fiction is a big place, really. It contains many countries. It is robust, it is healthy. Let them love and write. Let us each, in our ways, attempt to dignify our art and celebrate the wonders of the worlds of the imagination. The universe is large; I think there is room for all of us out there.

JE: How do you respond to the criticism that if you were as proud of your books as you suggest, you would put your name on them and associate with them more personally?

JN: I originally chose a pseudonym, as I stated, to protect my position in an academic institution. I also mentioned that "John Norman," in my opinion, is an excellent writing name. Further, my own name, John Lange, is used, or has been used, by at least one other writer as a pseudonym. Michael Crichton, for example, has used it. Indeed, one science-fiction editor, without checking his facts with either Dr. Crichton or myself, which seems to be standard operating procedure with this fellow, identified us publicly in the pages of his magazine. I am still trying to straighten that one out, as, I suppose, is Dr. Crichton.

We are both satisfied to be ourselves. That Dr. Crichton used my name, incidentally, is, as far as I know, a matter of complete coincidence. Perhaps he is lucky I did not, by similar coincidence, choose the name Michael Crichton as a pseudonym. He is one-up in this exchange. My own name, incidentally, is apparently very difficult for native English speakers to pronounce. This is another reason against using it as a writing name. Lastly, there are two further reasons for not giving up the name "John Norman." First, the name is now well known and famous. It would seem a bit late to give it up now. And who would want to? It's a fine name. Secondly, I am a teacher. I think it is peda- gogically desirable not to be generally recognized by my students as a well- known writer. I think little of educational value would be served in the class- room if these two identities were conflated. I think it is easier for students to relate to me if I am to them only their professor and friend. Many students, of course, do know my pseudonym. They, however, respect my privacy and my desire to separate these two roles in my life. In this they have perhaps demon- strated more civility and human courtesy than certain individuals in the science- fiction community. With respect to the parts of your question that have to do with "pride" in my books and "associating" with them personally, I might say that I do not really feel pride so much in the books, as that I think highly of them, that I love them, and I am grateful that they permitted themselves to be written by me. In the case of the Gorean books, my emotions are more akin to humility and gratitude than pride. The books are like wonderful gifts. Can one be proud of receiving gifts? One can be happy, of course, and grateful that one has re- ceived them. With respect to "associating" with my books, I have never at- tempted to dissociate myself from them. I am, of course, an extremely shy person, perhaps almost pathologically shy. Accordingly, it would be very un- typical for me to go about calling attention to myself, as the author of the Gorean books, or, for that matter, about almost anything else. Like many authors, I am an introverted person; I find it difficult to meet new people, etc. Further, I tend to decline to enter into controversies with people; I just don't enjoy bitter- ness and acrimony. Perhaps some people enjoy such things, I don't. I would rather be working. Accordingly, I do not think I have failed to associate myself with my books so much as I have not gone out of my way to do so. This is parti- cularly understandable, or should be understandable, in view of the intense and almost pathological nature of some of the criticism that has been heaped upon them. Indeed, I have been personally belittled and slandered by individuals I do not even know, and who do not know me. Sometimes, I wonder seriously about the sanity and moral character of some of these individuals. When there are people frothing at the mouth, running about, eager to kick John Norman in the shins, I do not think John Norman is under an obligation to roll up his pants and announce his whereabouts. Let those who enjoy being kicked in the shins do that. I don't.

JE: Does it matter to you that many people seem to misunderstand your work—misinterpret your intentions?

JN: I am not one of these authors who cries a great deal about being mis- understood. I suspect most readers understand me fairly well, on one level or another. Obviously, one cannot expect a sharp fifteen-year-old boy to have the same meaning-fulfillment from a Gorean book as a gifted, mature executive; he simply has not yet had the necessary life experiences. On the other hand, hopefully, both of these readers will find their experiences stimulating and rewarding. Many readers have read the Gorean books several times; they have learned, I gather, that there is more to come back for. It is nice to have written books that can be read many times. There are interesting questions here, incidentally, about the concepts of understanding a work and of interpreting an author's intent. Obviously, a Gorean book is not a secret message or a communication in code. Similarly, the relation of an author's intent to a finished product is surely an obscure one. He may have had no clear intent. If he did, he might not have fulfilled it; he might have changed his mind somewhere; he may not remember what his intent was; his memory may be untrustworthy, etc. A work grows in its making. It can start dictating its own parts. Then what happens to the author's "intent?" The notion of "intent," it seems to me, is too conscious a notion; I am not sure it is all that useful as a category for understanding literature. What was the potter's intent when he started on the pot? Probably to make a terrific pot. That may be about it. Some critics, of course, seem to have been almost perversely slanderous in their reactions to the Gorean books, over-reacting in ways that seem quite out of proportion to the texts involved. Here, I gather, some raw nerve or weakness in their psyche must have been touched. Perhaps, in cases such as this, it is fair to speak of such things as "misinterpretation." On the other hand, perhaps what is involved is not even really misinterpretation, which seems to imply a serious but unsuccessful attempt to understand the materials involved. The reaction, perhaps, is not even intrinsically or cognitively related to the triggering materials. When one, at a party, for example, presents a plate of dates to a young lady, and simply says, "Have a date," and she vomits, one may be fairly sure that this reaction has more to do with the young lady than with you or the date.

JE: Finally, have you flirted with idea of "coming out"—talking about your books and your view of the genre in a more open manner?

JN: I do not have to "flirt" with the idea of "coming out," for, in my opinion, I have never been "in." I have been fairly available to the science-fiction community and have, over the years, on a number of occasions presented my views on various topics. This question, like a preceding one, is simply based on a mistaken assumption. On the other hand, I do, frankly, think it is not in an author's best interest to be too publicly evident. The work is important, not me. Once the work is published, the author, I think, is well-advised to let it take care of itself. Hopefully, the Gorean books are not so obscure or incomprehensible as to require explanation and elucidation. Similarly, it seems to me that it is not the author's business to comment on his work, but, rather, that that is the task of the critic. I have never responded directly to any critic, as a matter of policy, no matter how idiotic, confused, or asinine he may have been. I feel that any honest reader of intelligence, perception, and awareness can see through the superficial would-be put-downs of intellectual pee-wees. This is not, of course, to be construed as a criticism of serious critics who have attempted to come to grips with the Gorean phenomenon. I have not, too, of course, discussed the honest and serious attempts to understand the Gorean works. This, too, is a matter of policy with me. Accordingly, I have not in the past, and I do not intend in the future, to publicly defend or discuss the Gorean books. This is not because I am a secretive villain, but because I do not think such defense and discussion on an author's part is either necessary or judicious. Beyond this, of course, I am a shy person; it is thus natural for me to avoid publicity and the limelight. Perhaps I would be much better off if I had a robust zeal for public relations and self-advertisement; I do not know. Too, it must be admitted that I do not find controversy stimulating. I am simply not that kind of person; I would rather be working.

HUGH B. CAVE: MASTER OF VINTAGE HORROR

Born in Chester, England, in 1910, Hugh B. Cave came to the United States when he was five. He grew up in the Boston area, attending Brookline High and Boston University. Cave began writing while in high school, and as a teenager sold stories to *Brief Stories, Short Stories*, and other magazines. According to the author, his high school English teacher, Miss Celina Lewis, recognized his writing ability and gave him much encouragement. As he tells it: "When I began getting things published while still in school, darned if she didn't correct even my published work!"

Hugh Cave won a scholarship to Boston University in high school competition, but failed to graduate for two reasons, although he later went on to evening study at other colleges around New England. First, his father was run down and nearly killed by an out-of-control street car, leaving the family shattered. Second, he began to sell enough stories to go into full-time writing. At this point, he was mixing college with a part-time job with a Boston vanity publishing house, for which he was rewriting other people's manuscripts (at age nineteen!) to make them publishable, and helping to edit several small trade journals.

A gifted and prolific writer, Cave sold over 800 stories to the pulps, spanning virtually every major genre—fantasy, weird-menace, detective, adventure, western, adult—appearing in all of the well-known pulp publications, as well as most of the lesser-known ones: *Strange Tales, Oriental Stories, Adventure, Weird Tales, Top-Notch, Terror Tales, Dime Mystery Magazine, Thrilling Adventure, Nickel Western* and *Spicy Mystery Stories*, among others.

By the time World War II broke out, Hugh B. Cave had moved from the pulps to the slicks. During the War, the author was a correspondent writing magazine pieces and war books. After the conflict ended, Cave spent five years in Haiti, where he wrote *Haiti: Highroad to Adventure*, a book that several critics have described as "the best report on voodoo in English." According to the author, "Haiti was the place that called me the most. With the popular response to my war books, I had no trouble getting a contract to do a book about that country. I went there in 1949 with my wife and sons intending to stay just a few months, but became deeply interested in voodoo and the few months added up—with, of course, comings and goings—to about five years, with other long visits after I stopped calling the place my second home."

In the course of his travels, Hugh Cave visited Jamaica, which inspired a well-received book on that country. The intended brief sojourn to Jamaica turned into an eighteen-year-stay, for in the course of exploring the island he stumbled on an old, rundown slave plantation which at one time had won various European awards for producing the world's finest coffee (Jamaican Blue Mountain). Cave converted its 541 acres of wilderness into a once-again successful coffee plantation and pine forest.

After the War, the author moved into the slickpaper market, producing countless short stories, novelettes, and even serials for such popular publications as *Saturday Evening Post, Good Housekeeping, American, Redbook, Cosmopolitan, Esquire, Liberty, Ladies' Home Journal* and *Country Gentleman*, to list only a few. In addition to his previously-mentioned pulp sales, Cave sold nearly 350 stories to the slick magazines and published a number of major books: *Drums of Revolt, The Cross on the Drum, Black Sun, The Mission, The Witching Lands, Run Shadow Run, Larks Will Sing, Long Were the Nights, The Fightin'est Ship, Wings Across the World, I Took the Sky Road, Four*

Paths to Paradise, and several others.

In 1967, Hugh Cave sold his Warwick, Rhode Island home and bought a condominium in Pompano Beach, Florida, in order to cut down the time and expense of travel between the United States and Jamaica. Then in 1975, with the shift of government policy in Jamaica and repeated warnings by those in power that foreign ownership of property was undesirable, he reluctantly sold the coffee plantation. Sadly, he had intended to retire there when his writing days were over, but the best laid plans . . .

About this time, with most of his old periodical markets out of business, Cave faced either retirement or a shift to some other kind of writing. The "some other kind" of writing that most appealed to him was the field in which he had been so successful as a very young writer—fantasy. It wasn't long until things began to break for Cave. The author recounts the story this way: "I began a novel, the first one I had attempted in a long time. It was a good one, I think, but it had to do with a character or characters who could swim interminably under water without needing air, and just when I finished it, damned if something called *The Man from Atlantis* didn't appear on television dealing with a character who could swim interminably under water without needing air!" The book in question, *The Human Inclusion*, hasn't yet found a publisher, but will some day when "Atlantis" is forgotten, perhaps. Meanwhile, Cave's next book sold to Avon, his next to Dell, and his agent thinks his latest, *Mission to Margal*, is his best yet. Moreover Carcosa Press recently published twenty-six of his best horror tales, *Murgunstrumm and Others*, for which he won the Best Collection award at the Fourth World Fantasy Convention in Fort Worth, Texas.

Today, Hugh Cave lives in Lake Placid, Florida, where he has actively resumed his career as one of the genre's master fantasy writers. He continues to work part of everyday at his typewriter, penning one successful novel after another. The author writes in a converted bedroom, overlooking an expanse of water, part of a golf course, and lots of green grass and trees, the same kind of rural atmosphere he cherished in Jamaica where his coffee plantation was at the very end of the last jeep road into the Blue Mountains. Asked to describe his work environment, Cave comments: "My workroom includes a closet for all the junk a writer accumulates. It has bookcases for a writer's books—my own and those I've collected over the years on subjects of interest to me. It has a nice wall in front of my desk on which I hang chapter outlines, character cards, things to remember to include in upcoming chapters of the novel in progress— all that kind of thing. And on the wall behind me, as I type, is a portrait I myself painted of an old Haitian friend, Maman Lorgina, the grande dame of voodoo *mambos* when I lived there. She is dead now, but I sometimes get the feeling she is looking over my shoulder when I write about the things she did."

JE: Consider the following passage from "The Brotherhood of Blood": "They call me an author. Perhaps I was; and yet the words I gave to the world were not, and could not be, the true thoughts which hovered in my mind. I had studied—and studied things which the average man dares not even to consider. The occult—life after death—spiritualism—call it what you will. I had written about such things, but in guarded phrases, calculated to divulge only those elementary truths which laymen should be told." How much of Hugh B. Cave is embodied in this passage?

HBC: Were "The Brotherhood of Blood" a more recent story, I'd be tempted to say there is a whole lot of Hugh B. Cave in those lines. I've spent the best part of five years in Haiti, studying and writing about voodoo. Indeed, *Haiti: Highroad to Adventure* was highly praised by several critics; *The Cross on the Drum*, a voodoo novel, was a double bookclub selection. I also published a voodoo novel in England, *Drums of Revolt*, and wrote quite a few stories on voodoo and related subjects for the *Saturday Evening Post, Collier's, American,* and other slicks. Then I bought "Arnually" in Jamaica—an old, 541-acre plantation in the Blue Mountains, and spent eighteen years restoring it—and a good portion of all the wages I paid out in those eighteen years went most certainly to local obeah people, one of whom, for four of the eighteen years, was also my housekeeper! In Haiti, I had an interesting housekeeper for a time, too. When boiling an egg, she invariably filled the pot to the brim with water. Then when the egg was done, she simply put her bare hand into the boiling water and lifted it out. It didn't surprise me much when she later told me she was a *hounsi kanzo* and, to become one, had had to put her hand into the seven pots of boiling oil. So, as I say, were "Brotherhood" a recent story . . . but it isn't. In fact, it's the first fantasy I ever tried. Before that, I had written for some of the adventure pulps and considered *Weird Tales* beyond my reach. In this regard, Farnsworth Wright bought "Brotherhood," asked for some minor changes, and gave it the cover of the May, 1932 issue, though it was the first thing I had ever sent him. I suppose, then, that the story was developed less from any personal beliefs of mine—I didn't have any such beliefs then—than from what I had been reading. I had certainly been reading fantasy. Lord Dunsany was a favorite of mine. So were H. Rider Haggard, Ambrose Bierce, Edgar Rice Burroughs, as well as the short stories of Rudyard Kipling, Robert Louis Stevenson, and *Weird Tales* itself. I remember seeing a production of Lord Dunsany's short play, "A Night At an Inn," and being stuck-in-the-mind with it for months. And there was a juvenile adventure book I read as a kid, about two boys who, fleeing from African savages, got into a cave, built a raft on an underground river, and for days or weeks drifted down that lightless river through "the bowels of the earth," encountering weird serpents and other creatures and never knowing whether they would get out. I believe it was called, *River of Darkness*, but I have no idea now who the author was. But the book made a tremendous impression on me at an early age. I wish I could find it again. Anyway, I was twenty-two when "Brotherhood" was published. I hadn't done anything much with my own life at that time, so the story couldn't have contained anything very personal. Later writings *have* put forth personal ideas of mine, especially my conviction that many of the mysteries of West Indian voodoo, obeah, zombiism, etc., won't be explained until we have more knowledge about such things than we have now.

JE: Why did you initially choose to write for the horror and detective pulps? What made you later move into other areas, such as adventure and western fiction?

HBC: I'm not sure that I wrote more for the horror and detective pulps than for other markets. Since I no longer have any of those old stories or even a record of them—lost them in a fire—I can't check on this, though out of pure curiosity I would like to be able to do so. I know I wrote a lot for *Short Stories, Argosy, Top Notch, Popular Fiction,* and *Oriental Stories,* to name just a few. The fact is, we "professional" pulp writers simply couldn't afford to specialize. Rates were low, and a writer who tried to stay alive by doing only one kind of story was in trouble. Look at some of the familiar names from those days and you'll see that all of them, or nearly all, wrote many different kinds of tales. And, face it, many of us were trying to move up to the slicks, to such magazines as the *Post, Collier's, American*, etc., where the better money was. To those writers, the pulps were merely a learning ground, a means to an end, and concentrating on any one kind of pulp story might be self defeating.

JE: What were the distinguishing features of the horror fiction you penned so skillfully and prolifically during this period?

HBC: I'd like to think it was the "craftmanship" Karl Wagner talks about—because, face it, much of the stuff in the old pulps was pretty shoddy. There were so many pulps, needing such a lot of copy, and, after all, not that many writers. Editors had to buy things they didn't want to, I'm sure. Those of us who were using the pulps as a stepping-stone to the slicks—who were really working to learn the craft of writing—must have turned out some of the better copy or we wouldn't have made it into such magazines as the *Saturday Evening Post*, would we? In his book, *The Shudder Pulps*, Robert Kenneth Jones writes about me: "His tales built up slowly and suspensefully to a final harrowing scene. He roved adept at this, although he modestly explains that he 'just plugged away, trying to learn how to write by writing.' " I remember my first version of the story, "Dead Man's Belt," which Karl Wagner describes as "a heralded classic from the golden age of *Weird Tales*." It was not a fantasy as I first wrote it, but an attempt at a slickpaper story. An amateurish attempt, no doubt—or should the word be "innocent"?—because what slick magazine would ever have used a story about two black men and a black woman living together in a big-city dump? However, that story, wide of the mark as it was, won me a "come again" letter from every slickpaper editor I mailed it to, and undoubtedly led to later slick sales. Then when it outlived its usefulness, I rewrote it as a horror story and Farnsworth Wright ran it in *Weird Tales*. But—you see what I mean about constantly trying to write something better than the run-of-the-mill pulp?

JE: What explains your tremendous popularity during the pulp era? Are you surprised by the current interest in many of your early pulp tales?

HBC: In writing to me about the possibility of collecting some of these old stories of mine in a book or books, Karl Wagner wrote: "Your stories were head and shoulders over the bulk of the weird-menace field; considering how fast you must have turned them out, it's astonishing how well crafted they were. Stories like 'Death Stalks the Night' are classic examples of the pulp formula, and display far superior writing than was usually given this type of story. 'Murgunstrumm,' which you did for the last issue of *Strange Tales*, I would consider a classic . . . paced with a relentless ferocity that few writers have ever brought off." Thank you, Karl, but the fact is, "Murgunstrumm" was never reprinted until your Carcosa Press reprinted it. Nor were most of the other tales in *Murgunstrumm and Others*. As for the rest of my pulp output, it hasn't yet resurfaced and probably won't, though more than seventy anthologies or school books contain reprints of my slick magazine stories. The fact is, most of today's fantasy readers had never heard of Hugh B. Cave until Karl Wagner began making noises about him. Whether I was "tremendously popular" during the pulp era, as you suggest, I don't know. No editor actually ever told me I was, but then, editors didn't say such things in those days for fear a writer would demand a hike in rates. They bought my stories as fast as I could write them, published them almost without editorial change because—I guess—it was my habit to send clean copy. I lived in Rhode Island then. I stayed away from New York because I disliked the place. I personally met only one or two of the editors who bought my copy. But I was young, worked hard, loved to write, and was a full-time freelancer, attending college nights, by the time

I was nineteen.

JE: Do you ever miss the days of *Weird Tales?* Do you have fond memories of that period?

HBC: No. I don't miss the days of *Weird Tales.* For one thing, though I enjoyed writing fantasy or horror or whatever it should be called, I had my eye on the slicks all that time—kept trying to break into them—and knowing the slicks almost never used fantasy of any kind, I soon began to concentrate on some of the adventure, detective and western pulps. *Then* I moved into books and the slicks, and it was only a couple of years ago that I returned to fantasy, this time with novels rather than short things. I had been a regular with the *Saturday Evening Post* for years. It folded, as did *American Magazine* and *Country Gentleman*, other steady markets of mine. I somehow got locked into *Good Housekeeping*, doing shorts and gothic novelettes. Then a new editor came on the scene and I thought of putting the typewriter away in the closet. But Karl Wagner wrote to ask if Carcosa Press could publish a collection of my old fantasy writings. And *Whispers* magazine asked for some shorts. All at once I was back in the past, at my first love, fantasy. Then, much to my surprise, *Murgunstrumm and Others* won the Best Collection award at the Fourth World Fantasy Convention in Fort Worth, Texas—the first such convention I had ever attended. I was so sure the book wouldn't win that I turned up at the awards banquet in a sport shirt, no tie or jacket, and had to go up on the platform that way to accept the Lovecraft statuette. My God—those old tales of mine, written forty-five years ago, were up against the best of *today's* writing. I was numb for a week. Incidentally, had I been called on to rewrite those stories, I would have thrown some of them out and made the book shorter. But Karl Wagner, bless him, must have known what he was doing when he selected them. He usually does. After that, I found myself doing fantasy novels, and having them accepted. However, I don't think I want to do many short things again. I prefer the long jobs, at which I can nibble away for a few hours each day with no one looking over my shoulder.

JE: The book jacket of *Murgunstrumm and Others* describes the stories as being exemplary of the gothic thrillers of the 1930s. Have those stories, in your opinion, withstood the passage of time? In what ways has the horror genre changed most significantly since the 1930s?

HBC: Some have, perhaps, but probably not very many. About three times a year, on the average, stories of mine from such magazines as *American, Saturday Evening Post, Good Housekeeping*, and similar slicks get reprinted in anthologies or school books. The only pulp stories that have survived seem to be the fantasies. *Murgunstrumm and Others* is a collection of those, of course; others have been reprinted in some of the fantasy magazines. Carcosa Press is planning a second collection of my old horror stories, or "dark fantasies" as they are now called, from such publications as *Terror Tales, Horror Stories, Dime Mystery Magazine*, etc. How has the horror genre changed since the days when I was writing for the pulps? Mainly for the better, surely. Today's writing is better; most of the stories being printed—except, of course, in the amateur fanzines—are more complex and sophisticated. We know more about fantasy subjects. There is a whole new world of fantasy "science" to draw upon, and the simple, basic conflicts can now be replaced with more subtle mental conflicts. Some of those old pulp tales were so simple they were silly. The danger now, I think, is in making a story so complex it becomes obscure.

JE: In the foreword to your book, *Murgunstrumm and Others*, you state that you chose not to change the old stories in order to improve them, that you could have made some stories more readable by reworking them today, but that that would have destroyed their authenticity. What kinds of changes could you have made? How could you have made the stories more readable?

HBC: Sure, I could have made some of those stories better. The title story itself made me wince with its repetitions of the word "lurid." I was also taken aback by the heaviness of some of its descriptions, although one reviewer—Jack Young in *Nightshade* #5—observes: "The title story is a vampiric master-piece, not so much because of the subject matter but because of the atmosphere. The yarn's strength lies in Cave's power of description. The images seem to shift in and out in a kind of black and white haze." Thank you, Jack Young, but after more than 350 stories in the *Post, Good Housekeeping, Liberty, American* and *Country Gentleman*, I have come to believe that overwriting is a sin. This includes overwriting even of the kind indulged in by H. P. Lovecraft, bless him for his original ideas. And so I feel, rightly or wrongly, that I could have improved all those stories in *Murgunstrumm and Others* by editing them down, tossing out some of the adjectives, and sharpening the dialogue. But, as I said in the foreword, they wouldn't have been authentic after such tampering, would they? They were written, remember, when rates were extremely low and a kid writer trying to be a professional had to make a typewriter smoke in order to keep eating. And that's how they should be remembered—for exactly what they were—if they are to have any social value in this day and age.

JE: How does "Ladies in Waiting," the newest story included in *Murgunstrumm and Others*, differ from the earlier stories? How would you compare that story, a 1975 haunted-house tale, with "The Whisperers," a 1942 haunted-house story? Has your approach or style changed in any notable ways?

HBC: "Ladies in Waiting" was written for Stuart Schiff's publication, *Whispers* magazine. I wrote it while alone in my plantation house in the mountains of Jamaica, just to find out whether I could still write the sort of thing I had done when I first got out of high school and began earning a living as a writer. Karl Wagner had suggested putting some of my old pulp fantasies into a book, which, of course, became *Murgunstrumm and Others*. His friend, David Drake, had asked if I wouldn't try a story for *Whispers* magazine, of which he was assistant editor. I sent Dave one that had appeared only in England and a couple of foreign countries. They used it. I was sick to death of writing for *Good Housekeeping*, which had been buying short stories and gothic novelettes from me for ten years (thirty-four in all). So one dark, rainy night, with the housekeeper gone home and no one in the house and the power plant chugging away to provide light, I sat down and did a first draft of "Ladies in Waiting." Next day, I rewrote it and mailed it off to Dave. They bought it. Karl reprinted it in *Murgunstrumm and Others*. Stuart Schiff also used it, I might add, in his Doubleday anthology called *Whispers*. Okay, I could still write the stuff. Wonderful. The day after I received *Whispers'* letter telling me it was real vintage Cave horror, I began a horror novel, and never again sent a story to *Good Housekeeping*, which was my last slickpaper market. Ah, freedom. How was "Ladies in Waiting" different from my old pulp horror stories? As a result of having written fifteen books and 350 slickpaper shorts, novelettes and serials, I learned at least a little more about handling characters and dialogue, how to set up a story's background, and how to plant information so the reader would say at the end, "Aha, why the hell didn't I catch that?" You be the judge of whether my style or approach has changed. I've always been a lousy judge of my own work. The best book I ever wrote—in my opinion—is still parked in my files, unpublished.

JE: Consider this passage from "Island of Dark Magic": "All these stories I knew to be greatly exaggerated, because my people were superstitious children at best. But I knew, too, that there must be some truth in them, for natives are not deliberate liars unless they can by lying gain material things for themselves." Is this an accurate assessment of island folklore? Is there evidence to support many native beliefs?

HBC: Yes. This passage is very much an accurate assessment of island "logic," but I don't know where I learned it from in those early *Weird Tales* days. I was born in England of a mother who was born in India. Her father built the great Indian Peninsula Railway and was Mayor of Bombay. My father was an English army officer who served in Africa. I heard about "the natives" all the time I was growing up, and probably based my stories on those tales. Also, I was fascinated by the South Seas—read every book I could find about that region—and probably subconsciously used much of that material, too. Later, I went there as a war correspondent, seeing at first hand the Solomons, New Guinea, Borneo, the Sulus, Iwo Jima, the Philippines, and other places I had so avidly read about. The fact is, though, that my parents were right. When I lived in the West Indies, I found out very quickly that "*li pa lwen*" in Creole, meaning "it isn't far," could be what they thought you wanted to hear. Or, "it only a likkle way" in Jamaican *patois* could mean it was just as distant. As for the truth of their beliefs, or whether they are purely superstition, I can only say, "Who knows?" after a total of nearly twenty-five years in the islands, and tell you the following story. My Jamaican housekeeper has a daughter, age thirteen. The girl was admired by a boy in her school class. He was killed by a bus while walking a rural road. Soon afterward, the daughter began to feel she was "haunted" by this boy, who appeared in dreams to her night after night. She was taken by her mother to "a woman who knew about such things." This woman stripped her naked, tenderly bathed her, talked to her, and after three or four such visits succeeded in "exorcising" the ghost of the boy who loved her, so that she could again sleep at night without nightmares, screaming, sobbing, and feeling worn out in the morning. Is this superstition? I have known this child since she was eight years old, and she is entirely normal. I pay for her upkeep and schooling, have talked to some of her teachers, and know she is one of the brightest in her class. Her teachers are as fond of her as I am. What's more, she didn't even *like* the boy who was killed, so there could have been no traumatic reaction to his death. You be the judge.

JE: As one who has invested much of his life in the study of voodoo, do you place considerable credence in its professed power? What are your experiences with it?

HBC: There isn't time here for a discussion of voodoo in depth, but it includes a belief in gods of various abilities, in possession by the spirits of those gods, in one's power to perform certain feats while so possessed. I have written about voodoo beliefs and practices in at least five books and don't feel I have even nicked the surface. Do I believe in it? No, not all of it. I do believe I have seen things done—by people I knew well, who had no reason to be trying to deceive me—that could not be explained. I have attended many different kinds of voodoo gatherings, in different parts of the country. I wore out four jeeps exploring Haiti, made many muleback trips into the roadless back country, even walked across the Massif du Sud—wild country with no roads, trails, or even footpaths—from Tiburon to Jeremie. All these journeys included attendance at voodoo services, as well as voodoo contacts in ordinary dealings with folks along the way. But, as I remarked before, I'm not prepared to put my hands in boiling oil, or grasp a white-hot iron bar, or pick up a red-hot iron pot with my bare feet as is done in a *kanzo* service. Nor have I ever been, to my knowledge, really possessed.

JE: As you view it what could Americans learn from Haitian folklore? In what ways could it enhance our understanding of life and our perceptions of the nature of man?

HBC: We might learn much from Haitian folklore if we could open our minds a bit more. First, we send "scientists" down there to investigate voodoo and such. They learn little because their approach is wrong. I came to know the best-loved *mambo* in all Haiti simply by arriving at her *caille* one night to observe a ceremony, at her invitation, and finding she was ill, trying to help her by driving all over hell in the middle of the night to get the right medicine. Since then I have been able to attend any voodoo ceremony in Haiti by using her name, even though she is now dead, and by knowing enough about her to convince others I was truly her friend. Go down there as a "scientist" to investigate voodoo and you have problems. Go live there with an open mind, as I did, and you may eventually be invited to participate in some of the most secret ceremonies. I was in Rhode Island one time when this same *Lorgina* sent word to invite me to participate in *La Souvenance*, a ceremony that takes place at Easter each year in a secret country village of fifty or so peasant huts, surrounded by a fence, which at all other times is abandoned except for a special caretaker. So far as I know, no other outsider has ever taken part in *La Souvenance*, a week-long affair restricted to the *mambos* and *houngans* of Dahomey origin in memory of their homeland rituals. Can we learn from this? I think we can. But hardly in the way we are trying to go about it, with hurried scholars going there for a week or two of research. Go live there a few years, get to know the people and their language, and you may learn more.

JE: The concept of "spiritualism" looms large in many of your stories. How would you define the term and what role does it play in your work?

HBC: I'll stick to the dictionary definition of "spiritualism"—the belief that the dead are able to communicate in one way or another with the living. I've written several stories based on this theme (e.g., "The Prophecy," which Karl Wagner calls a "*tour de force*"), but I don't think I've ever really believed in it, except perhaps in connection, once again, with things I've witnessed in the islands. I saw an eight-year-old boy drink a fifth of *clairin* once at a voodoo ceremony. That's raw rum, first distillation, and this bottle was a *trompe* in which red hot peppers had been steeped for weeks. The boy was possessed by the "spirit" of Guede, the voodoo god of death, but even so, downing a fifth of this fiery alcohol should have destroyed him. It did seem to make him a little drunk, but in five minutes he was just a normal child again, cold sober, sitting beside me and assuring me in Creole that he didn't remember what he had done. When I tasted the dregs in the bottle myself, a while later, it gave me a sore throat for days. So . . . I believe the evidence of spiritual communication that I've witnessed at many such voodoo services and similar affairs in the islands, but I am sure it is a thing beyond the reach of most of us, including myself.

JE: As you note in "The Prophecy," non-believers do not belong in the world of "spiritualism." Is spiritualism a dangerous area for a non-believer to venture into? What personal risks are involved?

HBC: Let me sketch you a picture here. You're visiting Haiti and someone who knows that country and its people invites you to accompany him to a voodoo service. It's night. You find yourself ten or twenty miles outside Port-au-Prince, say, at a peasant house on a dark country road where the yard is full of people and the scene is lit by lanterns. If this is one of the *tonnelles* set up for tourists, you can behave any way you like, within reasons, because you'll be paying for it and they are paid performers. But if it is a genuine service and you walk in among these people the way some tourists occasionally do at the commercial gatherings—disdainful, loud, perhaps even drunk—you will surely be asked to leave. Then if you become arrogant and refuse to leave, it can be dangerous for you. When I wrote "The Prophecy," a long, long time ago, I suppose I was trying to depict some of the different attitudes toward spiritualism that were in vogue at that time. I seem to remember that a group of us gathered in my Pawtucket, Rhode Island apartment, talked that way, and later that night did go to a spiritualism meeting where I secretly scribbled the notes I used later in writing the story.

JE: You've said that you believe in some, but not all, of the island practices you've written about. Is your primary goal to entertain the reader, or do you also seek to educate him in certain areas, such as those already mentioned?

HBC: All I want to do is entertain. If in writing about the West Indies, voodoo, obeah, zombiism, etc.—things I may know a little more about than the reader—I can also provide a bit of "education," fine. I believe what I've seen, and if I can't explain it, I say so. This doesn't mean, of course, that I have actually witnessed everything that takes place in my novels. Fantasy is fantasy. But my stories take place in real settings, and I like to think the fantasies in them are based on possible truths. You *can*, you know, imagine a three-inch lizard growing into a dragon and threatening to devour you.

JE: Do you have a particular audience in mind when you write fantasy? What does the reader look for in your work? Do you attempt to fulfill these expectations?

HBC: I don't know that I have any particular audience in mind when writing fantasy. It doesn't have to be slanted in the way that, say, a story for *Good Housekeeping* must be slanted. I'm not even sure who reads the stuff, but I suspect all kinds of persons do, from school kids to bank presidents. This was true even in the old days, I think. I always just did the best I could with the idea in hand. It never occurred to me to "write down" (can anyone really "write down?") just because pulp readers were supposed to be less informed than those who read meatier stuff. I suppose when a reader picks up something of mine, he's hoping for a good yarn and—these days—rather expects it to contain something along occult lines. I certainly try to provide the good reading, and somehow or other, if it's a fantasy, the occult sneaks in anyway.

JE: Must you be in a particular mood to write horror? What type of mental outlook is required? Is your working environment psychologically important?

HBC: I've been writing since I was in high school. I began by writing for the Brookline (Massachusetts) High School *Sagamore*, and have spent my whole life writing. Now and then the mind goes blank and the ideas dry up, but usually I can roll a sheet of paper into the typewriter and just start tapping the keys. This is so whether the product is a horror story or a letter to Aunt Minnie. Time and place have never meant anything to me. The room can be silent as a tomb or filled with music—jazz or Mahler. I'm very grateful for this, and have enjoyed the blessing all my life. The one thing I've never been able to do is dictate. I tried it once, wrote and sold one story that way, but realized I have to watch the words appearing on the paper in front of me or I lose all feel for what I am doing. Manly Wade Wellman, now a good friend, tells me with a chuckle that he met me once about that time and I even talked like someone who was trying to dictate.

JE: What types of people do you most enjoy writing about in your fantasy? Manly Wade Wellman, for example, often writes about country folk. You seem to employ a rich variety of characters. Do you have specific character preferences?

HBC: I really don't specialize in any particular type of character. If I have a preference, I probably lean toward the type of person I would have liked to be, myself: the curious, adventurous, independent kind of fellow who pokes his nose into offbeat places. Come to think of it, the leading characters in my books have been people of that sort rather than, say, men in gray flannel suits.

JE: Are there topics that you consider to be taboo in the fantasy-horror genre? What are the parameters of acceptability? When does a story border on "bad taste?"

HBC: My feelings along this line must have changed over the years, for I'm pretty sure I would not write a "Murgunstrumm" today. That is, I wouldn't have a physically repulsive innkeeper cutting up dead females and feeding the flesh to his guests as steak. I would not do a "Chain Saw Massacre" either—too much violence and gore. Maybe I'm just getting older. On the other hand, I no longer think, as apparently I sometimes used to, that blood and gore are necessary props in a horror story. Almost all the horror-menace yarns contained torture scenes; just look at some of those old covers on *Terror Tales, Horror Stories*, and *Dime Mystery*! Now, I think you can hit the reader harder with more subtle things, and there's no need to play the game of brinkmanship with good taste. This is true in novels, too, though a novel is long enough to allow for brief passages of almost anything.

JE: Given your military background and your penchant for fantasy writing, have you even considered writing heroic fantasy on the order of Karl Wagner? Is war a good subject for fantasy or horror, or are the horrors of war too apparent?

HBC: I've never felt I could do what Karl Wagner does. First of all, he does a tremendous amount of background research before writing his heroic fantasy. I'm sixty-nine years old and haven't the time. Besides, I know the islands. I know Haiti and speak Creole. I know Jamaica and speak the *patois*. My world is mine; his world of early England or whatever is a thing he has absorbed because he loves it. I may have been born in England, but I feel more at home in a mountain hut in Haiti or a peasant hut in Jamaica. As for war, I want no more of it. As a correspondent, I wrote a number of war books. *Long Were the Nights*, a best-seller for six months, was about the first PT boats at Guadalcanal. *The Fighten'est Ship* was the story of the cruiser "Helena" that was torpedoed in Kula Gulf. *I Took the Sky Road* was a book I wrote with Commander Bus Miller, the navy's most decorated aviator, who happened also to be one of the sweetest guys I've ever known, God bless him. I also did war books about the Seabees and the Air Transport Command. Let me tell you a story. I was on an LCI in the Strait of Makassar, en route with the U.S. Navy to support the Australian Silent Seventh Division in their attempt to retake Balikpapan in Borneo. (They took it!) One night in that dark, spooky silence I've been talking about, a PT boat pulled up alongside our slow-moving craft and a voice through a bullhorn called out, "Is Hugh Cave aboard there?" Well, as it happened, I was playing poker with Dalton Trumbo and George Harmon Coxe and a couple of other writers down below at the time, all of us grousing because the light was dim and the food inedible, so somebody came below and got me. And when I said, "Yes, this is Cave, who are you?" the bullhorn voice said, "We've got a book for you, Hugh" and somebody tossed a plastic bag onto the LCI's deck, and in it, so help me God, was a copy of my book, *Long Were the Nights*, about the PT squadron that had kept the Japanese from retaking Guadalcanal when we still didn't have a big-ship navy there. And in it—one of the proudest days of my life—was written by the men who had officered that squadron: "Dear Hugh, a swell book and a damn fine story of the squadron. Congratulations! (signed) Monty. Thanks for telling it the way we wanted it (signed) Bob. It turned out the way I hoped, Hugh. You can be proud of a fine job (signed) Nick." So . . . I feel I've written enough about war, and it's time to move on to other things.

JE: Speaking of the horror genre, what frightens you? Does your own work ever give you bad dreams? Do you ever test your work on anyone for impact?

HBC: I was scared half to death when a mule I was riding nearly plunged head first over a 200-foot-cliff in the mountains of Haiti. I used this incident in my book, *Mission to Margal*. Again, I was scared in World War II when a Japanese with a machine gun, trying to kill me, shot out the headlights and front tires of a jeep under which I had dived for cover. I dream a lot, and some of the dreams are a bit spooky, but whether it's my writing that induces them, I don't know. Occasionally, a dream fragment can be used in a story, but I don't recall ever having been able to use a whole dream. Yes, I sometimes test my work on others for effect, either reading it to them or asking them to read it themselves and comment on it. In Jamaica, I've read West Indian stories, even a novel, to my Jamaican housekeeper, to study her reactions to certain occult passages. "No, Mr. Cave," she might say, "a person would not say that to an obeah man. Wouldn't dare." Or, "There are other things to be afraid of while walking a lonely country road at night," and I'd be told about the things that might frighten *her*.

JE: One device you employ in several stories is that of "footsteps." Obviously, it serves to create an atmosphere of fear. How would you define "fear?" What makes something fearful? How do you evoke fear in the reader?

HBC: I love footsteps. On three or four occasions in real life they have scared the hell out of me. Once in Pawtucket, Rhode Island, I had to leave my car at a friend's house and walk home through deserted streets at 3:00 a.m. Footsteps followed me the whole way and there was no one behind me. I suppose it was something my shoes were doing, but I've never forgotten it. Once, when a correspondent on the island of Morotai in the South Pacific, I went along a jungle path, just exploring, and the same thing happened. This time it was probably a Japanese soldier (we had taken the island, but there were still Japanese in hiding) hoping to "win" himself a pair of shoes, but it was frightening. I am sensitive to sounds, perhaps from having lived in some quiet places. I've been told I often use sounds in my stories to evoke fear, but actually I suppose one automatically calls upon personal experiences when seeking to arouse any particular emotion in the reader. As for fear in general, I think the quiet things are the most effective—small sounds, loneliness, darkness, certain odors, anticipation of danger, and, above all, mood. Not violence, though. Violence may further the plot or settle an issue; it doesn't beget the kind of fear we're discussing here.

JE: In almost every horror tale, the protagonist could conceivably go mad, what with the bizarre and ghoulish things that occur. How often do you permit this to happen? For the story's sake, is it important that the characters come out of the experience whole?

HBC: Having someone go mad because of what happens in a horror story is an old, old device, it seems to me. I'm sure Poe used it. I know I have, both in the old *Weird Tales* days and more recently in a story written for *Whispers*

Magazine. Having the protagonist go nuts is a different thing, though, isn't it? It's probably not a good idea, though I'm sure it, too, has been done often.

JE: In your story, "Watcher in the Green Room," you advance the idea that man creates his own monsters from his own thoughts. This would seem to come far closer to reality than many storybook monsters. Do you strive to incorporate a psychological viewpoint into your work? Is there more reality to your writing than meets the eye?

HBC: Yes. Indeed, this is one of my favorite themes now. I hadn't been aware that it went back to "Watcher in the Green Room," which appeared in *Weird Tales* when I was only twenty-three years old. It would seem that in "The Watcher" I was anticipating the kind of horror story that is now taking the place of the old pulp tale of raw violence, perhaps. At any rate, I have just finished a new novel, *Mission to Margal*, which I mentioned earlier, and in which assorted ideas of this kind are carried out in depth. Here, we seem to be getting back to my answer to a previous question, in which I tried to say that a character can be more frightened by what his mind is doing to him than by the sight of, say, some purely physical act of violence. In *Mission to Margal*, for example, a woman is asleep in a peasant hut in the mountains of Haiti. She is awakened by the rustling of a lizard in the thatch above her bed. The lizard drops onto the bed to devour a glow bug. Her mind, in a way discussed later, changes the lizard into a thing the size of a crocodile that seems to devour *her*, and she is terrified in a way no mere witnessing of an act of violence could terrify her. To me, this is the new horror story, and I'll be doing more of it.

JE: Revenge is a powerful motive in "Murgunstrumm" and "Horror in Wax," two of your most popular horror tales. Is revenge an effective horror device?

HBC: Yes. I think revenge is an excellent horror device if you can make your reader believe it. I used it in my recent book, *Nebulon Horror*; it's part of what makes the kids tear the town apart. I don't think it's enough by itself, though. The ordinary reader has probably never in his life felt any strong desire to "get even" with anyone. I tuck it in there as an added motivation.

JE: In several of your stories, notably "Prey of the Nightborn" and "Horror in Wax," you mix love with horror. What role does love play in your horror tales? Is there a place for sex?

HBC: If a horror story is about people, it must inevitably show them as loving people or sexy people. The whole idea is to make them real to the reader. In a recent book of mine, *Legion of the Dead*, my hero is a man just divorced from a sexless wife. He visits a college friend in San Marlo, where he meets the lovely, sexy, eighteen-year-old daughter of an ex-prostitute. They walk across the mountains together to escape danger, making love all the way. Some people who've read the book say this is the best part of it. Yet the book itself is a horror-fantasy about a Caribbean dictator who employs an army of zombies to keep himself in power, and it contains a full share of fantasy, or horror, and no small amount of violence. Fantasy has come of age. It requires real people, doing real things, or it's going to have a Wonderland feel and all the characters will be Alice.

JE: In your collection, *Murgunstrumm and Others*, most of your stories feature male protagonists. In many cases, the female characters might be described as "sex objects, complete with firm, round ivory breasts." Is this not a chauvinistic treatment of women? Do females ever play leading roles in your horror fiction?

HBC: The stories in *Murgunstrumm and Others* in which the gals are described as having "firm, round ivory breasts," are those from *Spicy Mystery Magazine.* I doubt you are familiar with the "Spicy Group," but they were considered quite sexy in their day. No one ever *did* anything sexy, but the ladies had to be described at every opportunity. In stories other than those written for this group, I believe my women were reasonably normal, except, of course, most of the pulp magazines I wrote for featured male leads. In this regard, I didn't write for the so-called "women's pulps," such as *Love Story.* On moving into the slicks, I did a number of stories in which women or girls played the leading roles, and several of these were pretty popular. One, "Extra Girl," from the *Saturday Evening Post*, has been reprinted a number of times in anthologies. Another, "Danger by Night," from *Today's Woman*, was done on television, with David Niven playing the part of her husband. There are, of course, lots of women in my novels.

JE: Members of the medical community are notorious skeptics (Karl Wagner excluded!) Doctors play a pivotal role in several of your horror tales, among them "Murgunstrumm," "The Brotherhood of Blood," and "Maxon's Mistress." Is medical skepticism an effective horror technique? Is it a useful springboard from which to advance ideas about unexplained phenomena?

HBC: I suppose doctors creep into horror stories more than other kinds of tales because other characters need them for treatment after encountering the ghosties, monsters, or whatever. In that sense, they are certainly useful, and their medical skepticism would seem a natural device for furthering the suspense.

JE: Like most fantasy-horror writers, you've written your fair share of tales about vampires. How many ways can a vampire story be told? Do you run the risk of cliche with tales involving subjects, such as vampires, haunted houses, monsters, and such? How do you avoid this pitfall?

HBC: I'm just about convinced that all vampire stories, including the half dozen or so that I have perpetrated, are merely copies of *Dracula.* Well, perhaps not "copies" but "extensions." I won't be writing any more of them for the simple reason that I can't think of any way out of the rut—or should I say out of the coffin? With haunted houses, monsters and such, the risk of cliche is not so great, because these things are less restricting. I can think of a hundred different jollies that could be set against the background of a haunted house, and a fair number of monsters that haven't yet been created. But Dracula, the Frankenstein monster, the Wolf Man, the Mummy—these are too well defined and too well known. For me, that is. Other writers may feel there is still some blood in these old corpses.

JE: To what extent does a book or magazine illustration enhance the effectiveness of a horror story? Are monsters and corpses best left to the imagination? Does detailed illustration detract from the power of a tale?

HBC: That's a touchy question. My collection, *Murgunstrumm and Others*, was illustrated by one of the best horror artists in the business, for which he won a World Fantasy award for his drawings. I think his pictures in the book are absolutely tops. However, when I'm reading a story, I don't always appreciate having an illustration there to shape my idea of what the writer is saying. This is especially true where it concerns a fantasy creature. I think, as you suggest, that monsters, corpses, ghosts and such are best left to the reader's imagination. Yet, some of Lee Brown Coye's haunted houses—especially the inn in "Murgunstrumm"—knock this opinion of mine to a cocked hat. And that picture of the rat on the table, with "Arthur loves Betsy" carved in the table-top . . . oh, brother!

JE: What advice would you give to upcoming fantasy-horror writers? Are there still many untapped story ideas or are the classic themes the most profitable?

HBC: The whole field of study in psychic phenomena is constantly expanding, and I would try to keep up with it, just as science-fiction writers try to keep abreast of new developments in their field. The classic fantasy-horror themes are stale now. I try to avoid them.

JE: Finally, what kinds of writing are you doing today? Are you writing any new fantasy novels? What other projects interest you at the present time? What do you have scheduled for future publication?

HBC: I'm writing several fantasy novels. Perhaps that's the wrong word, because they aren't the J. R. R. Tolkien kind of thing, but stories of fantasy-terror laid against real backgrounds I'm familiar with, such as the West Indies, Florida, and New England. My book, *Legion of the Dead*, was recently published by Avon. As I mentioned, it's about a Caribbean dictator who uses an army of zombies to stay in power. From Dell is *The Nebulon Horror*, about a gang of possessed kids who take over a small Florida town. Karl Wagner has a collection of my weird-menace yarns from the old *Horror Stories, Terror Tales, Dime Mystery Magazine*, etc., and Longman's Ltd., has a collection of my *Good Housekeeping* short stories for use in English classes worldwide. I've also recently completed the Haitian voodoo-sorcery novel, *Mission to Margal*, which I discussed earlier. In the typewriter is a Florida-Jamaica tale of sorcery and obeah which ought to keep me busy for the next four or five months. Meanwhile, Stuart Schiff has a couple of my short stories, one of which he is using in his Doubleday anthology *Whispers II*, while the other was bought for his magazine.

KATHERINE KURTZ:
TAPESTRIES OF MEDIEVAL WONDER

Katherine Kurtz boasts a background as creative and varied as her fantasy novels—the trilogy "Chronicles of the Deryni": *Deryni Rising, Deryni Checkmate, High Deryni*—and *Camber of Culdi, Saint Camber, Camber the Heretic*, the "Camber trilogy." One of the most popular series in print, the Derynan stories are sweeping tales of romance and sorcery set in the imaginary kingdom of Gwynedd. For both series, Ms. Kurtz draws heavily on her background in medieval history, weaving wondrous tales of magic and adventure.

The author was born in Coral Gables, Florida, during a hurricane—a whirlwind entry into the world which she likes to think was an omen of things to come. Kurtz's acquaintance with the written word began early in life. Indeed, Katherine's acquaintance with the written word began early in life. Indeed, her mother began reading to her from the time she was an infant in arms. She was a natural mimic, and on her second birthday, so she is told, she recited the entire poem of "Little Orphan Annie" for her grandparents, without a mistake or a hesitation. "I don't remember a time," recalls Kurtz, "when I couldn't read. I do know that I was already reading by the time I started school at age five, and was at the top of my group, the Bluebirds (lower reading groups being Redbirds and Yellowbirds)."

Elementary school held few challenges for Kurtz. She used to take library books to school and hide them under her school books, so that she could read what she wanted in class, to keep from getting bored. "I believe it was in the third grade," remembers Kurtz, "that I persuaded the librarians to let me have the run of the school library, instead of being confined to the picture books usually reserved for lower elementary school students. The clincher was the day I wanted to check out a copy of Walter Farley's *Black Stallion*, and they didn't want me to; they said it was too hard. I proceeded to open it and read, and they asked me a few questions about what I'd read. From that day on, I was allowed to check out as many books as I wanted, from whatever section I wanted. I also began reading out of the local city library."

Kurtz read her first science-fiction book in the fourth grade. It was a juvenile called *Lodestar*. From then on, no science-fiction book in the library was far from her reach. Even then, though, her tastes were geared toward humanistic science fiction, rather than hard science stories. According to the author, "Technology and bug-eyed-monster stories never appealed to me, and still don't. I preferred ESP themes and strong characters. I also got away from short stories more and more. I've always felt that short stories, for the most part, constituted cruel and unusual punishment for the reader; because if they're good, you no sooner get going and they're over; and if they're bad, you've had to wade through all these little snippets of bad."

Kurtz's high school education was better than most. She graduated from Coral Gables High School, which, at the time, was one of the top five or so high schools in the country, especially in the sciences. She was a regional semi-finalist in the Westinghouse Science Talent Search her senior year, and that recognition won her a four-year science scholarship to the University of Miami. As she views it now: "I suppose you could say that the science award was my first really big break, because without that, I couldn't have afforded to go to college and God knows what I'd be doing now."

The author's preoccupation with science didn't last very long once she hit college. True, she graduated with a B.S. in Chemistry, and even attended medical school at the University of Miami for a year, but her heart had been lost to the humanities and, especially, history, during her freshman year. As an undergraduate, she honed her writing and research skills on strict academic writing, so that by the time she came to the conscious choice to quit medical school and return to academic study, she had all the formal tools necessary for the transition. The short story which eventually became *Deryni Rising* was written during her senior year at the University of Miami. She wrote several *Star Trek* scripts the year following her withdrawal from medical school, mostly as learning exercises; and by the time she moved to California to continue her graduate studies in history, she was well enough along in the transitional process to begin writing serious fiction. The rest of her writing career is fairly well known, not to mention remarkable: a three-book contract with Ballantine Books with the first try, the initial books now well into seventh and eighth printings, with subsequent ones headed in that direction, and a faithful fan following which seems to be ensuring that the books will continue to be written and bought with gratifying regularity. Now, at last, ten years after she signed her first contract, Kurtz is finally making the transition to full-time writing, taking a leave of absence from her present position as a designer of instructional materials for the Los Angeles Police Academy, to see whether she can make it as a full-time author, money-wise. "It's a great joy," confesses Kurtz, "even if it is a little scary."

JE: Can you state how you found your way into writing? When did you first aspire to write? How did this interest take root?

KK: I've always enjoyed writing. I started out as a reader. I was a voracious reader. I think I started reading when I was around four or five, and I've never stopped. I can remember in elementary school, which was *not* sufficient challenge for me, taking books to school and hiding them in my desk, lifting up the lid to read a page or two when the teacher wasn't looking; or hiding a novel under a textbook. And then, there were those innumerable nights when I'd read under the covers with a flashlight. I think most writers have gone through that stage. Anyway, having been brought up on reading, I suppose it was natural that I reached the point when I thought, "I could write a story better than that." And eventually, I did learn to do that. But in the meantime, I served my apprenticeship as an academic writer. Very early on in my student career, I learned the rudiments of good research practice, strict academic writing—like, never, never use a contraction. Never, never write an incomplete sentence. Of course, a lot of these things are elements that have to be overcome when one switches from academic writing to writing fiction. But the discipline of academic writing was a good thing, I think. I despair of young writers coming up today, who haven't had the benefit of that strong background of grammar and spelling and punctuation. One can argue that those things don't matter, in the face of true artistic genius; but I maintain that your young genius is never going to get his deathless prose read, if the potential editor has to wade through pages of sloppy, misspelled, non-grammatical prose. The material may be very good—but presentation is important, too. An editor has too much to read, to take the time to wade through something that is going to ruin his or her eyesight faster than it's already getting ruined. The aspiring professional should be aware that first impressions *are* important.

JE: Who most encouraged your early interest in writing? How important was this encouragement in the formative stages of your career?

KK: As for my own development as a fiction writer, that was, in some respects, a long time in coming. My formal academic training was as a scientist. I was pre-med through four years of undergraduate study, and even started medical school. This kind of curriculum leaves one very little time for reading, much less writing, fiction. Fortunately, I had the good sense or the good fortune to take a very large number of courses in liberal arts disciplines, as well as sciences, even though I was working toward a B.S. degree. My professors in the humanities encouraged my creative endeavors; and one in particular, Mr. Carl Selle, even predicted that I would one day be a writer, not the physician I consciously thought I was going to be. You see, we were kindred spirits. He'd been where I was then. He'd started out as a medical student, too—though he only lasted one day, while I stayed for a year. When I quit medical school and went back to graduate school the following fall, I saw him during registration and told him what I was doing, that he'd been right. Unfortunately, he died before I actually began my writing career; but at least he knew I was back on the right track. I dedicated the first book, *Deryni Rising*, to him.

JE: For the past several years, you've worked closely with the Los Angeles Police Department, as an instructional technologist. Do you still work full-time for the City? Is there a good possibility that you will soon be turning to writing on a full-time basis?

KK: I made the decision to write seriously, I suppose, during that year of medical school, when I really began to realize that my creative time was going to be curtailed more and more, over the next few years. And then, in that next year, while I worked full-time and went to graduate school part-time to recoup my finances, I really began working on my fiction in earnest. I don't know when I made the decision to make the writing come first. I suppose that's been evolving for a long time, since I've been working full-time at another job for the past ten years while I've been building my reputation as a writer. The most difficult decision is coming up in the very near future, when I make my break with the world of salaries and shift to writing full-time. It's both exciting and scary, to consider living on a six-month-income schedule instead of an every-two-weeks one, but it's what I've been working toward for more than ten years now, and the positive aspects far outweigh the negative ones. I'm looking forward to it.

JE: What initially provoked your interest in things medieval? What makes this period so personally fascinating?

KK: Oddly enough, I never had any real interest in the Middle Ages, historically speaking, until I hit college; and I don't know that it would have happened then, if I hadn't been in an honors humanities program. Somehow, public school education manages to kill history for most kids by turning it into a dull, boring compendium of dates and facts. The way most history is taught, one would never know that it's about real people who lived and loved and created and thought—not just battles and wars and reigns of kings. In any case, I encountered a very uncommon professor the second semester of my freshman year. His name was John Knoblock, and he was and is a professor of philosophy at the University of Miami. He was also the first true genius I'd ever met; at that time, he was about twenty-two or twenty-three, with a brand-new Ph.D. in oriental philosophy and art. He was also a proponent of the then-new concept of teaching history and all the other areas covered in the humanities by an integrated approach. The time period that we covered was from the fall of the Roman Empire up to the Renaissance—but it wasn't a compendium of boring dates and facts—not at all. We studied the art, the architecture, the music, the poetry, the religion—all presented so that it related, each area to the other. He would bring in slides illustrating the points of architecture, for example, and ask us to tell him whether a window was Romanesque or Gothic, and why. He taught us about the feature of later artwork which he called "the Renaissance point." Take a look at almost any Renaissance painting, especially if it shows more than one person—religious themes are particularly good for this—and you'll notice that all of the lesser characters are pointing at whatever it is that's the center of attention in the painting: the crucified Christ, Pilate washing his hands, the Virgin Mary holding the Child. This was indicative of the tenor of the times, that if the artist didn't make sure you noticed the subject of the painting, by having the people point at it, you might not get it. And these characters would go into all kinds of weird poses, uncomfortable and sometimes anatomically dubious ones, to get that finger pointing at the most important person. I think it was the architecture that really pulled me into medieval history, though. That may sound strange, but consider that architecture reflects the needs and the ways of thinking of the people. Church architecture, for example, went from the old Roman basilica form to the basic Romanesque design, sturdy and solid (to protect against the barbarian incursions), and on to the more soaring Gothic period, as life became more stable and man was able to have the time to turn his thoughts to God, instead of just worrying so much about mere survival. By the Gothic period, just prior to the true Renaissance, we have the flourishing of the cult of the Virgin, which also contributed to the whole troubadour-trouvere movement. (You didn't think *all* of those troubadour songs and lays were dedicated to mortal women, did you?) Anyway, getting into the architecture and its whys and wherefores got me into the philosophy and religion. And as anyone knows who has read the Deryni books, that became a major interest for me in the coming years—and still is. As Henry II puts it in "Becket," I became involved in the *aesthetics* of the Church; and gradually, this intellectual fascination with that whole mythos became something far more spiritual. Nowadays, I read straight history and philosophy and religion for pleasure, as much as I read fiction—probably more. I'm especially fascinated by the way man's search for Deity has taken so many forms, and how the whole concept, in all its differences of belief and practice, somehow dovetails in a coherent whole. I don't think that any religion with a positive orientation is basically in conflict with any other one of like nature; I don't think there's any one, right, true religion, either. Each person has to find his God—or Goddess—in his or her own way; and that Deity is going to be a little different for each person, regardless of the fact that it may be possible and comforting to band together with other people of similar beliefs for public celebration. Religion—one's relation to the Creative Force—has to be a very personal thing. It isn't something that can be dictated by someone else—though formal religion can certainly suggest various frameworks within which to structure one's belief system. This may sound like a bit of a contradiction, considering the role the Church plays in the Deryni world; but if you'll think about it, you'll realize that most of the characters who consider themselves religious have a definite and personal way of looking at the Church. They choose to operate within the general framework most of the time, but they have different ways of thinking, on an individual basis. Camber's God, for example, is silent a great deal of the time—or maybe Camber just isn't listening on the proper frequency—but He is basically an understanding and forgiving God; Cinhil's God, on the other hand, is wrathful and punishing. After all, didn't He make Cinhil's son Javan deformed, with that club foot, as a sign of His displeasure at Cinhil leaving His priesthood? That's what Cinhil thinks, anyway.

JE: To what extent did your academic training, a Master of Arts degree in medieval English history from the University of California at Los Angeles, prepare you to write epic fantasy?

KK: I had actually started writing epic fantasy long before I started my graduate work at UCLA, so I don't think it was so much a matter of my M.A. work "preparing" me in that area. It was good leavening along the way, though, since it continued to hone my research skills and exposed me to actual medieval records more in-depth than I would have managed on my own. My graduate seminar project, for example, had to do with translating the Hundred Rolls from Bedford County in England. These related to an inquiry conducted by Edward I in 1274, when he came back from the Crusades to find out what his ministers and Crown officers had been doing with his country while he was absent. The records I was working with were in medieval Latin, and done in an abbreviated form which meant that you had to expand each contraction to its full Latin form before you could ever begin translating—and my Latin, at that point, was limited to what I'd learned from Church Latin. Fortunately, much of the wording was somewhat formulized—these were charges brought against sheriffs and other Crown officials by the Hundreds, or sections of the country— and so it was fairly easy going, once I'd mastered the abbreviations and the formula phrases. I came up with a fascinating picture of local corruption at various levels of government that I'd love to follow up someday by finding the rest of the records about this inquiry. These were only the charges; I never got to see the other side. I do know that there's a fascinating historical novel in there someplace. I'd call it *The Sheriff*, and it would tell of this medieval sheriff, who's been taking a little on the side and turning his head while his subordinates rip the people off, who suddenly realizes that the King is coming home and the sheriff is going to have to answer for what he's done. One of these days, in my copious spare time . . . .

JE: When asked which author most influenced your approach to writing fantasy, you cited Frank Herbert and his classic novel, *Dune*. What did Herbert teach you about the genre? Did he influence your attitude toward writing? What about the actual process itself?

KK: I think what impressed me most about *Dune*, at the time, was the deft handling of characterization. I studied the way Herbert made his characters interact, how he wove together dialogue and action so that it flowed. There were very few slow spots in *Dune*, even when the characters were only talking. He had a very visual style in that book, and that was the way I wanted to write. I actually took apart a few of his scenes and analyzed them for this unique blend of talk and action which was successful for him in that particular book, so that I could figure out how he did it. I don't think I've ever done that with any other book, at least in writing, though there will be scenes here and there that I'll stop to reread, to appreciate the artistry which makes a particular scene outstandingly successful. But Herbert was only a jumping-off point, so far as learning that particular lesson. Far more useful, in terms of sheer craftsmanship, was writing *Star Trek* scripts back in 1968—and I heartily recommend this kind of exercise to any writer who's still trying to perfect his or her dialogue and pacing sense. The idea is to take a television series that you particularly like—*Star Trek* was ideal, since it had very strongly realized characters and a good, solid universe to work with—and to write a sample script for it. Format is not particularly important for the exercise—though, if you pick a show that's going to be on the air for a while, there's always the chance (granted, slim) that you might be able to sell the script. What is important is that: first, you have to fit your story into a somewhat artificial but disciplined structure of a teaser and four approximately equal length acts, each ending on a cliffhanger or other note that will make the reader want to come back after the commercials (the same principle applies to chapter endings); and second, you already know how the characters talk, how they phrase things, so you can worry about writing believable dialogue which will carry your plot, instead of having also to worry about whether the character will hold together. (It can be extremely difficult to keep all the points in mind at once, when you're just starting out; hence, you concentrate on just a few things, at first.) From there, it's much easier to ease into writing one's own material, with original characters and universes.

JE: Unlike most fantasy writers, you achieved professional status almost overnight, going from an unpublished writer to a writer with a contract for three books. Can you relate the events which led to the sale of the Deryni trilogy?

KK: I guess I was too naive to realize that people don't sell three-book contracts their first time out. I had written a short story, "Lords of Sorandor," while I was still in college, and when I came to California, I started toying with the idea of expanding it into a novel. When I went to Baycon, the World Science Fiction Convention in Oakland in 1968—my first science-fiction convention, ever—I met a man named Stephen Whitfield, who had written the very successful *The Making of Star Trek*, for Ballantine Books. We got to talking, and I told him about my idea, and he said, "Hey, Ballantine is just beginning to look for original fantasy for their new Adult Fantasy series. Your idea sounds like it would be perfect. But don't write one book; write a trilogy." "You've got to be kidding," I said. "I haven't even written one, and you want me to write three?" "No problem," he replied. "What you do is, you write the first few chapters of the first book, with a page per chapter outline of the rest, and then you write a paragraph or so about each of the other two books. I'll tell Betty Ballantine to expect it." Well, after several gulps, and many questions, all delivered in a very small, timid voice, I decided that maybe I could do it, after all. I didn't have enough experience to realize that the odds were almost astronomical against such a thing succeeding. So I wrote my outline and my sample chapters and I sent them off—and two weeks later, got back that magical letter from Ballantine saying, "Hey, we really love your idea, and how does a contract for three books sound, with thus-and-so terms?" Talk about being blown away. Anyway, I accepted—and then settled down and began to work in earnest on *Deryni Rising*. It was well received, especially for a first novel, and I continued working on *Deryni Checkmate* and *High Deryni*. By the time those were finished, I had begun to establish a small but loyal following among fantasy and science-fiction readers. And when I started the Camber Trilogy, things really started to take off. With the third and final Camber book, *Camber the Heretic*, the del Reys and I mapped out at least six books in the Deryni universe. We've also talked about a mainstream novel which has the potential to be a bestseller, and I'm working on closing a contract for a film version of *Deryni Rising*.

JE: As you assess your present situation, has this instant rise to professional status proved to be a totally positive thing—that is, would you be a better writer today had you been required to serve an apprenticeship? Where was your training-ground to fail?

KK: I think my experience has been a positive thing. There are still times, though, when I sort of stand back and look at how far I've come and think, "Wow, is this really me?" Though I've had to work full-time at another job while I've been getting myself established as an author, I still am in the unusual position of actually making a living doing what I love to do—and unfortunately, not too many people are able to do that. Hopefully, I will be able to do what I love to do—writing my own things full-time. As for a training-ground to fail, I think I've had that; I've just not had it as public as many writers do, since I don't do short stories, as a rule. There's one, "Swords Against the Marluk," in *Flashing Swords #4*, but that's really part of a novel that I'll be getting around to in the next year or two.) I think that authors who go the short story route get much more accustomed to the chanciness of writing. A novelist does his or her work in much larger chunks, so there's more time to work out glitches and more chance that a good editor will catch you before you go to press and make you fix the awful things that might get through in a short story. I'm not knocking short stories; I just don't care for them. I don't like to read them, and I don't particularly like to write them—and the same reason holds for both dislikes. Perhaps it's a lack of discipline, but I can't seem to confine myself to that short a format. My ideas are just too big, and I feel constricted by having to squash them down. I don't like to read them, either, because just when a story starts getting good, it's over. So I avoid short stories, for the most part. (And having said that, I have to tell you that I will probably be doing one sometime, since an incident has come up in the novel, *Camber the Heretic*, which doesn't fit there, but wants to be told. So I will probably write it.) I have had my failures, by the way, both in science fiction. One was a short story that I wrote as a favor to a friend, and then he didn't like it for the anthology he was putting together. The other was a science-fiction novel that I did for a publisher which shall remain anonymous, to the publisher's formula, and which, when finished, didn't match the formula which the publisher *then* said was what we'd agreed on. And, of course, because the book had been written to a formula, it wasn't fit for anything else in that form, so I've done nothing further with it. Someday, I'll go back and do it the way I should have done it the first time; but for now, it's just stuck in a drawer. There's a good story there, though.

JE: You've described your particular brand of writing as "historical fantasy." What does this term imply?" How does it differ from what is commonly thought of as "fantasy" or "sword-and-sorcery?"

KK: I would describe "historical fantasy" as fiction which is set in a universe which closely corresponds to our own history, so far as sociological and religious background is concerned. In the Deryni books, I've tried to be very careful to give a real historical flavor to what I've written, drawing very heavily on my background as a cultural historian and trying to instruct as well as entertain. Very much of what I talk about, in terms of horses, falconry, sailing ships, food, armor, costume, etc., is drawn from our own historical background. The saints I mention, for example, are all pre-tenth century or else they're made up. When I ordained Camber in *Saint Camber*, I took the ordination from a technological level, such as giving Morgan's ship *Rhaffalia* a jib, which really wasn't developed until several hundred years later in our own world, I try to give a plausible explanation for the difference. In a way, my world is an alternate or parallel of our own, with the divergence probably having occurred about the fifth or sixth century. Regular fantasy does not pretend to parallel our own history, except in the broadest sense. It tends to be more fairy-tale medieval, for the most part, though it may draw heavily on mythological background of various cultures. And sword-and-sorcery is even more eclectic, tending toward more action and less characterization, in general, with magic that may be almost entirely of the hocus-pocus variety and inhabited by creatures which never walked the world we know, except, perhaps, in nightmares. I think that characterization and internalization are important to the kind of fiction that I like to read, and I think my writing shows this. Regular fantasy and sword-and-sorcery tend not to stress these points as much as I would like. I suppose that's one reason I started writing my own. Many writers get their start writing out of sheer preservation, because they can't find enough to read, of the type they want.

JE: How extensively do you draw on history in your fantasy, both for plot ideas and story details? What does history enable you to do, as a writer, that intuition doesn't?

KK: As an historian, I'm convinced that we can and should learn from our history, both the mistakes and the successes. But if a person hasn't studied history except as the series of dates and battles and royal reigns, such as we discussed earlier, then he may not be aware of the valuable lessons to be learned from history. So I am constantly on the lookout for points of history that have relevance today, and for those connections of philosophy which are universally valid, regardless of the outward trappings. Handled skillfully, these can be both entertaining and enlightening experiences for the reader, not to mention the writer who puts them all together. I learn things from every book I write. The research and the bringing together of all the elements are half the fun of creating. As for intuition, that is often the catalyst which takes two or three only-possibly related elements and from then synthesizes a new way of looking at something. Sometimes the characters themselves take the elements and forge something I wasn't expecting. Something magical happens when your characters start showing up at your story conferences with yourself. The first time Camber looked over my shoulder, I nearly fell out of my chair. Javan,

Cinhil's middle son, did that just the other night.

JE: One would imagine, upon reading your work, that you read and write Latin quite fluently. Is this the case? The Deryni fantasies make superb use of Latin terminology, but not to an excess. How do you know when to stop, when you're approaching overkill? What functions does the Latin serve in your fiction?

KK: I fake Latin very well. Most of the Latin used in the books is taken directly from the Latin Missal or other liturgical sources. I do read Latin reasonably well for the purposes of translating old records, but the rest comes from faking it, as I said. I also have several priest friends who bail me out, from time to time. They like the books, by the way. The purpose of using the Latin in the first place is partially to give the flavor of the times—after all, the medieval Church was a great, overshadowing influence on all walks of life, in the real middle ages. I guess I just have a good sense of balance, as to how much is enough but not too much. In the case of any strange word, I try to use it in a context so that the reader has at least an idea what it means. Then, if he looks it up, too, that's even better. But at least I've planted another word in his unconscious, and hopefully he's going to be the richer for it. All human endeavor can enrich others of the race. Even negative human acts can instruct and give us a better appreciation for the positive human values.

JE: The Deryni fantasies draw heavily on your background in medieval history, patterning the imaginary Kingdom of Gwynedd after ninth-century Wales. Why did you choose this specific time period? What about this period, from an historical viewpoint, makes it productive for such a series?

KK: Wales provides only a part of the background for the Deryni series. When I wrote the first book, I had never been to Great Britain, and I had this intellectual fascination with Wales that was based solely on what I had read and intuited about that fantastic country. When, between the completion of *Deryni Rising* and *Deryni Checkmate*, I actually went to Wales, that fascination was confirmed; but I also went to Scotland for the first time, and the Yorkshire area—and those really turned me on. If there's such a thing as reincarnation, and I tend to think there is, then I've been in Scotland before. Crossing the border was almost a physical sensation; it was like I'd gone home. Consequently, a lot more of Scottish and English flavor came into the later books, not just the Welsh influence. Lately, since I've been to Ireland and read more on the folklore and traditions of all these areas, my view of the Eleven Kingdoms has become even more eclectic. I think it makes for a much richer tapestry. As for time settings, I'm covering a two hundred year span just now, from around 916 to the early 1100s; and that's a period that's far enough removed in our own history that there's a great deal we don't know about it. That leaves me a lot of latitude in my speculations.

JE: What are some of the explicit and implicit assumptions which underlie the Deryni universe? Are they readily apparent in your fiction? How apparent do you try to make them?

KK: I would say that the most explicit assumption is that magic works, though this has several aspects. We can define "magic" as any occurrence which seems to operate by means which we can't explain, especially if there seems to be no causal connection supported by scientific evidence. It's also been defined as science not yet understood, as it might be viewed by superstitious, non-scientific people. Much of what the Deryni do, that's considered magical by their contemporaries, is what we are beginning to call science today: telepathy, telekinesis, teleportation, healing. They use hypnosis, too, though they have the added advantage of forcing a receptive state, which we do not, in this universe. Much of their so-called magical activity seems to take place within the trappings of what we might call "ceremonial magic," but there are also things which are mystical, bordering on the religious. And then, there are things which even they can't explain; they simply work "spells," and things happen. Of course, modern psycholgists would point out, and rightly, that the purpose of ritual is to achieve a certain mental set, to get one into the right "head-space" to be able to turn the mind loose to realize special potentials which are not normally accessible at the conscious level. And this is true. But understanding how a phenomenon works doesn't make it any less valid. Whether the "spells" which the Deryni use are simply mnemonic devices to trigger certain mental sets, short-hand procedures for previously used rituals, is not important. What is important is that these are ways which work, for them, for gaining access to these higher human potentials. The fact that the Deryni discovered that these potentials can be awakened in some humans simply illustrates my belief that we all have some of these potentials, to some extent, and that if one works at it, one can always become better than one was. In this, the Deryni are embarked upon the classic quest for the Philosopher's Stone, the aim of the ancient alchemists. It wasn't really to make gold out of lead; it was to refine the human spirit and make it more valuable than it started out, to burn away the dross and reveal the perfected man. Now, the Deryni are far from perfect, but they do understand the need for this constant quest for perfection, knowing that they can never *reach* it, but knowing, also, that if no one tries, no one will ever rise any higher than he is. They do the best they can, with what they have been given. And a man's reach must exceed his grasp, else what's a heaven for?

JE: Can you discuss the process of inventing an imaginary world, one that is both interesting and believable? How do you go about the actual task of constructing such a world?

KK: Constructing an imaginary world is both easier and more difficult than the uninitiated might think. A lot depends on how large a story you have to tell, how far-ranging you're going to be in your story-telling—a lot of things. For a world that's going to show up in more than one book, one almost has to have a map. I have one, and I try to be very scrupulous about putting new places on it, as I use them in the stories. This is the only way to avoid geographic inconsistencies. I also keep genealogies, since so many of my characters are related in some way; I keep lists of members of different groups, with ages and any distinctive features such as the color associated with their magic, if they're Deryni; drawings of ground plans of buildings where my characters spend a lot of time, especially if I plan for them to go back there again; coats of arms; places mentioned but not yet placed on the map; who's associated with what lands. I'd be lost if I didn't keep my lists. I also do time-lines of events, as I've found out that's the only way for me to keep my interwoven plots and subplots from getting hopelessly tangled. The key to the whole thing is consistency; and this is the key. I don't care what kind of world one is writing about.

JE: Do you do extensive research in the course of writing a novel? Is all your research of a library nature? Do you ever do any personal experiments in order to understand a problem you're writing about?

KK: I do some library research. I haunted the Loyola Library the week I was working on the scene in *Camber of Culdi* where Cinhil's first son is baptized. I didn't have a Latin translation of the ceremony at home, and I nearly went crazy finding one. I did a lot of that kind of research on excommunication and ordination, too. My references to horses are largely gleaned from actual experience, when it comes to talking about their behavior. As for experimentation, in a way, I've done some of that. I recall that when I was writing that scene in *Deryni Checkmate*, where Morgan has been drugged with Merasha and has fallen down the chute under St. Torin's shrine, and he's coming to—I got down on the floor and tried out that passage, to see what he really would have seen. Often, when I'm sitting at my typewriter, I'm making the facial expressions and gestures of my characters, as I write about them. Of course, all the background on hypnosis is authentic, too. My training as a hypnotist goes back many years, and my interest even farther. Hypnosis is not quite as versatile a tool for us as it is for the Deryni, but it's useful, nonetheless.

JE: The Deryni universe is clearly distinguished by your mastery of historical costuming. Have you read extensively in this area? Have you made many medieval costumes? Have you ever worn such costumes? Has your practical experience in this area enriched your fiction?

KK: I guess I've always been interested in costuming. I've always loved to wear costumes, and make them. Perhaps this goes back to having fairy tales read to me as a child, before I could even understand what my mother was saying. I'm told that she read to me from the time I was an infant in arms, and that on my second birthday, I recited the entire poem of "Little Orphan Annie" for my grandparents. Around elementary school age, the boy across the street and I (and later, my younger sister) used to play knights and queen, and we rode stick horses with intricate harnesses, and carried cardboard shields. I remember a yellow cloak made out of an old chenille bedspread. Of course, Florida was too hot and humid to do much in the way of dressing up outside, at least in the daytime, but I'd draw pictures at night, and tell my friend to imagine that this was how we really looked. It wasn't until I came to California and discovered the Society for Creative Anachronism (SCA) that I really discovered the joys of historical costuming. I learned to sew when I was around seven or eight, and long ago reached the point where I'm not afraid to tackle much of anything, so far as a sewing project is concerned. Sewing medieval clothing is a little different, though, since you don't work with patterns, in the usual sense. That took a little getting used to; and I've had my share of disasters, and done my share of ripping out. But making and wearing medievals, as we call them in the SCA, is still one of my favorite ways to unwind. And, of course, making and wearing these clothes teaches you a lot about what one could and could not do while wearing them, and the reasons for some of the design features. These range from use intended for the garment, type of fabric available, *width* of fabric available—for, you have to remember that in the very early medieval times, the size of the loom was limited, so when you had to hand-weave every piece of fabric, you were going to want to make optimum use of that piece, and you weren't going to want to cut it anymore than necessary. Remember that the lady of the manor was responsible for clothing the entire household. She might have ladies to help her with the spinning and weaving and sewing, but this was pretty much a year-round occupation, just keeping clothing on everybody's back. When you have to go through that, you use and re-use every scrap of fabric, and cut down adult clothing for the children, and so on. We re-cycle clothes today, too.

JE: There are at least three, if not more, major themes in your fantasy: first, there is nothing wrong with being different; different does not necessarily imply bad; second, power in itself is neither good nor evil; it is how one uses it; and third, it is not good to misuse the gifts one's been given; instead, one has an obligation to use them as wisely as possible. Could you explain each of these themes in the context of your fiction?

KK: I think you've stated the themes very well. The first theme gets down to the basic notion of prejudice, I suppose. We encounter all kinds of prejudice today—racial, religious, ethnic, social class. The point is, prejudice is so unfair. It isn't right to judge an individual on the basis of a group to which he belongs, especially if it's something over which he has no control. I suppose we could say that there are some areas of prejudice over which a person does have control, like religion or social class, since, at least in theory, a person could change his religion or make a million dollars and bring himself up to a better social class. But things like skin color, or Deryniness—these can't very well be changed. Furthermore, it isn't right to expect that people should have to change. None of these things I've mentioned hurt anybody else, in themselves. Certainly, things can be misused—but the qualities, in themselves, are neutral. As for the second theme, the amoral nature of power, it's the use of power which takes on moral coloring. Atomic energy is an obvious modern example: the bomb versus nuclear medicine. Or, to shade the judgment a little, a reactor which goes critical—power intended for good but gone astray—versus a well-run nuclear generator which benignly produces energy to power a whole state. Getting into the more human resources, we might use the example of a brilliant scientist doing research in bacteriology. He can look for a cure for cancer, or he can develop items for bacteriological warfare. The same genius, but turned to different ends. Among the Deryni, the contrasts are even more obvious, some of them using their enormous power to protect, some to destroy; some to heal, some to subvert the weak. Wencit of Torenth, for example, without his drive to regain what he felt was his, by whatever means possible, might have turned out quite differently. There was enormous power and potential there; yet he ended up as just so much cooling corpse—and it had to be that way. Finally, the theme of using one's gifts wisely. I think this is a definite area which carries over into our lives. Everyone has various potentials, but they have to be realized. First, one has to recognize that they've got these potentials; and then, one has to develop them. Cinhil is probably the best example in the books. He fights like hell to avoid doing and being what he was born to do and be. The problem with Cinhil is that he was born to do and be several things, and the society in which he lives can't handle him doing both. He's led a peaceful and fulfilling religious life for most of his years when we first encounter him. He's a good priest and contemplative. He could have spent the rest of his life behind the cloister walls, and been perfectly content. He probably would have made a positive contribution to the life of his religious community, too. But he's also a prince of the royal blood, the only one left. And there comes the time when the need for him in this other, secular role, is greater than the need for him to stay in his monastery. You'll recall that poignant conversation he has with Archbishop Anscom, the night he's to be married to Megan, in which the Archbishop points out the new duties which call. And Cinhil knows that Anscom is right, at least in his head. But he never manages to convince his heart, and that plagues him for the rest of his life, though he does attain a measure of personal fulfillment, once he resumes his priestly offices in private—especially once he confides in Alister-Camber and has someone with whom to share this aspect of his life.

JE: You've written extensively on the genetic code of Deryni inheritance. What is the basis of the code? How does it operate? What surprises does it hold?

KK: The notes on genetic aspects of Deryni inheritance were a first crack at figuring out how the powers are transmitted. In the beginning, I postulated the Haldane potential being carried on the Y chromosome, which would endow all males of the line with the capability to have Deryni-like abilities put on them. This is consistent with what I'd developed in the beginning, concerning the Haldanes. Genetically speaking, there's no reason that all Haldane males couldn't assume Deryni powers; but because they've been told that only the King can hold the power at any one time, they think that the others can't. We'll see, in a later book about Kelson, that this is not true. Conall will learn this lesson very tragically. This particular potential is only male-linked, so we won't see any women receiving a magical potential in this manner. As for actual Deryni inheritance, I had originally envisioned it as being a single factor transmitted on the X chromosome, but I've realized, since I wrote that original speculation on gentics, that there have to be multiple factors involved. We know, for example, that the Healing factor is a separate one, that not all Deryni can heal. In fact, only a small percentage of Deryni can heal. The Healing factor also seems to be preferential for males, though we'll see a few female Healers. Rhys and Evaine's fourth child, a daughter named Jerusha, will be a born Healer. But there are definitely multiple factors at work here, because even Rhys and Evaine's children aren't all Healers. Two of the four are—a boy and a girl. One of these days, I'm going to sit down and rework the genetic theory governing this. I suspect that the factors involved are more like the ones that determine eye color, for example. You can get different degrees of involvement. And, of course inherited Deryniness is definitely a potential. Born Deryni still have to be trained to realize their abilities. Otherwise, you get people like old Bethane, who learn just enough to be dangerous. We'll see a little of Gabrielite training of Deryni, some of them Healers, in *Camber the Heretic*. It's a shame the Gabrielites had to be wiped out, because they were really impressive people. We could use some of them around today.

JE: In the course of writing the Deryni fantasies, you've wrestled with the problem of logic and consistency. Is this a major worry in a series as vast and as complicated as yours?

KK: A lot depends on how large your concept is for the universe you're developing. Authors who set out to write one book, with no thoughts of continuing in that universe, tend to write themselves into corners and out of the possibility of sequels. If they later decide to do a sequel, they may have a rough time of it. *Dune Messiah* is a good example of this. Frank Herbert wrote a monumental masterpiece in *Dune*, but he wasn't thinking in terms of a sequel. By the time he went on to do *Dune Messiah*, he had a lot of corners to write himself out of, and the book suffers as a result. But he planned ahead for *Children of Dune*, and that book, while not as good as *Dune*, was infinitely better than *Dune Messiah*. Then there are authors who drive their readers crazy by not worrying whether every little detail is consistent from book to book, so long as each book is consistent within itself. Marion Zimmer Bradley, who is one of my very favorite people, does this a bit in her Darkover books, and it's certainly understandable, considering the vast time span over which she's written the books. Some of the inconsistencies she merely shrugs off. There's one, however, that I love, where she explains away a differing account by saying that this particular character was under a great deal of stress at the time a specific incident occurred, and he may not have remembered exactly how it happened, that his memory may have been mercifully blurred. It takes a rare and special talent to pull off that kind of escape from inconsistency, and Marion is an expert.

JE: In the course of reading the Deryni series, one cannot help but be impressed by the meticulous attention to detail (e.g., costuming). Is this talent an outgrowth of your training as an historian? Do you consider this a trademark of your writing? Is there the possible danger of loading the reader down with too much detail?

KK: I don't think my attention to detail is so much a product of my historical background as it is just a part of me. I'm a very visual person. I have a vivid imagination, especially for scenes and colors and sounds. Some people have commented that the opening of *Deryni Rising* reads as though written for the screen—which is interesting, since I'm in the process of selling that book to a major producer for a feature film. I didn't necessarily have that in mind when I wrote it, though. That's just the way I say it. If anything, it's the result of the scientific observation I was taught before I ever entertained the idea of being either an historian or a writer. Certainly, it's possible to go into too much detail. But it's not so much how *much* you tell, as *how* you tell it, that makes the difference. A good description, if it's properly balanced with action and dialogue, can be a great asset to creating the proper atmosphere in a story. If it's overdone, it can drag the whole thing down. Oddly enough, I've been criticized both for too much and not enough description. I suspect that the too-much advocates are the ones who are not strong visualizers themselves—and there's nothing wrong with that—and they really *do* get bogged down with too much detail that they just can't see in their minds' eyes. Early on in the books, about the time I was starting the Camber books, Lester del Rey called me on omitting some of that detail, though. As I recall, I'd talked about setting Wards Major many times, in the course of several books, and tried a short-hand description of what happens in the process. Lester came back and said, "Katherine, you have to remember that some of your readers are picking up any given book for the first time, and they may not have read the expanded version of what is old-hat to you, by now. Besides, they love your magic. They want it in all its details. So don't short-change them." He's right, of course. The trick is to retell those things that have become familiar to me, in ways that are fresh and won't bore me or my faithful readers, yet will still give that first-time excitement to the reader who is encountering it for the first time.

JE: Can you discuss the genesis of the Deryni series? Where did the idea first originate?

KK: The original idea for the series—or, I should say, the idea which later led to the Deryni concept—came from a dream I had back in about 1965. That was just the ghost of the story later told in *Deryni Rising*. Jehana was the one who had to assume the dead King's power, and Kelson was an infant in arms. There was also the possibility of a romantic interest between Morgan and Jehana. I wrote that in a short story called "Lords of Sorandor," which I've since published in the *Deryni Archives*, a magazine put out by some fans under my supervision. It was that story which I described to Stephen Whitfield, in an expanded version. And reading that story today, it's interesting to see what parts got translated almost intact in the final novel, and what things changed radically. I can't tell you where the Deryni themselves came from. They weren't in "Lords of Sorandor," at least by name. I wish I could remember how I discovered them, but it's been too long, and I've been too intimately involved with them for too long, to be able to recapture that discovery process. It really is more of a discovery process than a creative one, by the way. My readers have remarked, but not before I'd realized it myself, that at times, it's as though I'm recounting real history, not just telling a story I've made up.

It's enough to make one wonder if it isn't possible, perhaps, to tap into another dimension. Maybe there really *are* Deryni, somewhere, somewhen. When one of those characters takes a storyline and runs, it certainly seems like there's something at work besides mere imagination.

JE: Many avid readers of fantasy, particularly those who enjoy the Deryni series, can cite several very strong lead characters in your work. What makes characters, such as Morgan, or Duncan, or Cinhil, so memorable?

KK: I suppose the major difference between my characters and a lot of other fantasy characters is that mine are full of very human foibles and faults, even the heroes. By the time you've gotten to know a Morgan or a Duncan, you know a lot about what makes them tick. They're complex. And the heroes aren't all white, and the villains aren't all black. I'd say that the ones my readers identify most closely with are Morgan, of course, Duncan, Derry (which was something of a surprise to me, since he started out as a very minor character), Rhys, Evaine, and Camber. I feel closest to Camber, myself, with Duncan probably a close second. Camber is sort of a Deryni Thomas More, in many respects, with a lot of extra added attractions. He's an extremely ethical man who has to deal with situation-ethics a great deal of the time, and it bothers him, even though he really believes he's doing the right things for the right reasons. Cinhil is another character that I feel I know very well, though I don't like a lot of the things about him. He goes a long way, from the time we first see him living in his monastery, until he dies in *Camber the Heretic*. So does Camber, for that matter. Camber is very real for me. I'd know him if I ran into him on the street. (I should. He's peered over my shoulder at the typewriter often enough!) I'm very fond of Rhys, too, though I don't understand what makes him tick as well as I do Camber. And Evaine is like me in many respects, especially her passion for learning about things and solving puzzles.

JE: Speaking of your characters, one wonders how you went about selecting their names? Did you select names that were prominent in this period? Did you invent many of the names? How did they originate?

KK: I collect names. Whenever I go to a foreign country, I look for books on "What to Name Your Baby." I have them from England, Wales, Scotland, Cornwall, and Ireland, to name but a few. I like the Celtic flavor, and I like formal-sounding names. I hate nicknames, for the most part, especially the diminutives—Bobby, Johnny, Billy, Tommy. Yuch! The fastest way I know of to get my fur bristled the wrong way is to call me Kathy. So many people think they're indicating friendliness by calling a person by a nickname, even when they've been introduced by a given name. When I introduce myself as Katherine Kurtz, it's because I think of myself as Katherine, and I want to be called that. If I wanted to be called Kathy, I'd introduce myself that way. That's one of my few pet peeves. I always call someone by the name they want to be called. Names are very important. I would never name a child of mine a name that could be corrupted by unthinking clods—at least not a name that could have a diminutive ending put on it. My little nephew's name is Graham, for example. No way you're going to put a "y" ending on that and have it sound like a cutesy name. And I have a half sister named Brenda. Again, no way to shorten that badly. As for my characters' names, I use historical names and made-up ones. I'll often use a less common spelling, like Brion. Occasionlly, a character will address another by a shortened form, such as Alister addressing Jebediah as Jeb in a casual situation—but not a diminutive!

JE: Most science fiction and fantasy writers steer clear of religion as a major theme in their work. Yet, the Deryni fantasies are heavily steeped in religion, drawing extensively on custom, myth, ceremony, etc. Why do many writers in the field avoid this subject? Why do you place such important emphasis on religion? Do you have a particular view of religion or approach to religion that you attempt to incorporate into your writing?

KK: It isn't particularly surprising to me that science-fiction writers tend to steer clear of religion in their stories. I think the modern trend is to feel that somehow religion, especially in the realm of faith, is increasingly unimportant in the light of scientific sophistication. People brought up in a technological age, especially those with a strong scientific education, tend to distrust anything they can't see or measure. They view religion as the opiate of the masses, a psychological crutch which the progressed man doesn't need anymore. They think that organized religion, with its myths and customs and ceremonies, is out of date in these modern times. And if it's out of date now, it will surely be out of date in the future. Hence, when you encounter religion as a salient point in most science fiction, it's in the context of either a decadent civilization or a primitive planet where the progressed Earthmen are going to release the natives from theocratic bondage. Perhaps this is harsh judgment, and there are exceptions to this generalization, but this is my impression. Even when most science-fiction writers do try to deal with religion in a meaningful way, they come up short because they try to invent an alien religion without realizing what religion really means, and they aren't able to get into the emotional range of what religion is all about. The result is that the religions *do* come out as shallow and unsophisticated, thereby proving the writers' theories that religion is an unimportant appendage of human psychology, and not worthy of the sophisticated and educated modern man. Fortunately, some science-fiction writers do eventually reach the point of some of their really advanced scientist brothers and sisters, who have discovered that, in the long run, they *have* to acknowledge some universal Creative Force. Beyond a certain point, the most sophisticated scientists seem to come to the almost unanimous conclusion that there has to be Something to account for the majesty and order of the universe. This is basically a return to the foundation of religion, albeit in a more nebulous, less formal manner. Unfortunately, when most people reach this undeniable acknowledgement of that Great Something, when they've experienced the Great Awe, they become inarticulate about it. Theologians will write about it, but scientists generally don't. That's a shame, because I think they could give us some beautiful insights, from their unique point of view. I *am* surprised, though, that more fantasy writers don't deal with religion, since they tend to have a liberal (as opposed to a hard science) education, and should have been exposed to human history in greater depth than one would expect of a scientist. Given an historical orientation, it's almost impossible not to realize that the Church in the Middle Ages, especially, was the single, overpowering influence that touched the life of every man, woman and child, even more than kings and warriors. Since most fantasy writers draw heavily on a medieval or quasi-medieval background, it's amazing that so many of them ignore this important point. Again, perhaps it's because they're uncomfortable talking about something which is really so close to the human center, whether you're talking about Judeo-Christian religion or the gentler aspects of the Old Religions. Modern man doesn't often have time to seek a mystical experience; and I think this is reflected in what is being written today, not just in fantasy and science fiction, but in all kinds of literature. Drug culture used this quest for the mystical as an excuse for their activities, but drugs have a tendency to become the end rather than the means. Some people are discovering that a mind-high is much better than a drug-high, and with no nasty side-effects, but achieving this state only with your own head takes a lot more discipline and control than just popping a pill or lighting up a joint or shooting up something. I don't take drugs; I don't even like to take an aspirin unless it's really necessary. But I've had some experiences that were absolutely mind-boggling. The mystical experience is something that still gives me shivers of sheer awe. I suppose I've drawn a little on that in the Camber books, especially. Remember, I told you that there was a lot of me in Camber. I've used this religious approach in the Deryni books both because of the historical framework and because I guess I want to try to share a little of the magic of what religious experience can be. And if you put that kind of thing in a fantasy novel, people who ordinarily would be a little skittish about acknowledging this part of them, in their modern, scientific educations, are often able to taste it just a little. And some of them go on and explore further on their own. Religion can be the opiate of the masses, as some folks charge; but if you take it a few steps beyond dogma and get to the archetypal foundations, the mystery of existence, you can find something that is valid and has meaning, at different levels for different people. The outward form isn't that important. Personally, I'm most comfortable in a Judeo-Christian framework similar to what I describe in the books; but I can also be comfortable in any of a number of other frameworks. People may call their gods by different names, and acknowledge Him or Her in different ways; but it all goes back to the Source, in the end. There are many valid paths to the Godhead.

JE: Has the Deryni series bridged the gap between the fantasy audience and the mainstream audience? Are there tangible signs that mainstream readers are buying and enjoying the books? Do you aspire to branch out into other fields? If so, which ones?

KK: I think it has, to a certain extent. I've had reports that people who never read fantasy before have picked up my books and gotten hooked on them, and then started branching out to other fantasy and science fiction. People who like straight historical fiction also like the books. They've also been great for getting junior high and high school kids to start reading—kids who've never read a whole book before in their lives. I've had some amazing reports from teachers who use the books as catalysts for getting kids to read. I do plan to do other things besides the Deryni, though. I mentioned the book on the medieval sheriff. I also have a couple of mainstream-type projects that I'm going to do one of these days.

JE: Some critics have argued that the early Deryni books are not as deftly written as the later ones. Would you agree? If so, why?

KK: Of course, the earlier Deryni books are not written as deftly as the later ones. I wrote *Deryni Rising* in 1969; I was ten years younger and less experienced then. Also, *Deryni Rising* was a much simpler book, in terms of plot and characters, than any of the later ones. People don't usually realize, until I point it out to them, that *Deryni Rising* is very unusual in that it all takes place in little more than twenty-four hours, other than the opening chapter. There's just so much you can do in twenty-four hours, especially if it's a first novel and you're still finding your literary balance. If I were writing *Deryni Rising* today, there are some things I'd add; and when the film version eventually comes out, folks will see some things added. It doesn't change the basic story; but the script is much more the way the story would have gone, if I'd written it today. It's a bit expanded, shows a little more of the relationship between Morgan and Brion and Kelson. We actually see Morgan before he goes off to Cardosa, and a little of his relationship with Kelson. It's going to be great fun. As for progress, I would certainly hope that the later books are the better ones. If they aren't, it means that I haven't been learning my lessons as an author. I'm told, for example, that *Saint Camber* is the best one to date, and I have to agree. I like that book very much. I still reread passages from time to time and think to myself, "Wow, that's neat. Did I really write that?" And the neatest part of all is that I did! If I didn't enjoy writing so much, I wouldn't do it. It's nice that other people like to read what I've written, but if it didn't please me, too, I certainly wouldn't spend all those hours behind the typewriter.

JE: In what sense could it be said that you've grown as a writer? Can you see clear signs of improvement in your work? What do you do better today than when you began writing? What areas still require further effort?

KK: Language seems to be the thing that's criticized most by reviewers. They seem to think that fantasy has to be full of thee's and thou's and lots of archaic language. That can be good, if it's done well, but it can make a book limp along very badly if it isn't just right. From as objective a point as I can manage in answering that charge, I would have to say that I'm not J. R. R. Tolkien or C. S. Lewis, and I don't think it's valid to criticize the Deryni books because my language is not theirs. I try to keep blatant modernisms out of the language, but I *am* writing for modern readers, and communication is sometimes more important than formal style. There are those who can handle this epic language beautifully, and I admire them for it; but I don't think that the stories I have to tell would benefit from being couched in that form. I could cite Mary Stewart's Merlin books as beautiful examples of language handling. And there's a novel called *The White Hart*, by Nancy Springer, that was published by Pocket Books recently, that's marvelous. But I don't think either of these ladies could tell the Deryni stories as well as I can. Different kinds of tales call for different ways of telling. Still, I am aware of the fact that my language usage bothers some folks, and I'm trying to broaden the epic sweep of what I'm doing.

JE: Since your full-time profession is not writing, do you find sufficient time to write every day? Can you keep to any kind of set regimen? Does this haphazard approach impair your skill and/or productivity?

KK: Right now, it's difficult, if not impossible, to write every day. I probably average a couple of nights a week, and at least one day a weekend, with occasional bursts of writing binges when I'll turn out forty or fifty pages in a weekend. I can do editing during my lunch breaks at work, but it isn't the best way to try to write novels. I'm really looking forward to the day when I'll be able to write only what I want to write, and on the schedule I set. Hopefully, I'll be able to spend a certain amount of time each day reading and doing research, as well as writing, once the writing business is full-time.

JE: In recent years, writer-editor Lester del Rey has come in for considerable criticism, owing to what some critics have called his "crass commercial motives." On the other hand, you have said of del Rey: "I admire and respect him tremendously. I couldn't ask for a better mentor at this stage of my career." What explains the wide divergence of opinion surrounding del Rey?

KK: I don't know that much about the charges of "crass commercial motives" surrounding Lester. I do know that I've enjoyed working with him tremendously, and feel I've learned a great deal from him. I read a lot of his work during my formative years, and it's very satisfying to be working with him now, as I build my place in the genre. His instincts about the Deryni have been very good, for the most part, and the few disagreements we've had have always been resolved to the betterment of the books and in a manner which has not been personally negative for either of us. We like and respect each other as craftsmen. I can't imagine why there's such a wide divergence of opinion about him.

JE: Speaking of your fans, you state: "My fans have been very good to me. They have rewarded my attention to them with astonishing loyalty and devotion." How has this affection manifested itself? How does an author repay such a show of appreciation?

KK: Fans provide an author with positive feedback on his or her work. They also provide an interaction that isn't possible while the author is actually sitting behind the typewriter. This is important, especially when one occasionally runs into glitches and needs reassurances. Fans also give one different perspectives, which sometimes lead to new ideas. One of the things I've done recently is to work with a couple of Los Angeles fans to produce a Deryni magazine. I hesitate to call it a fanzine, since it's really more of a journal on things Deryni, and it's a bit higher caliber than the average fanzine. It's called *Deryni Archives*, and I think one of its most important functions is that it helps span the gap between books. Fans can get very anxious and impatient when they have to wait one-to-two years between books; but since that's the best I've been able to do, so far, the *Deryni Archives* provides a showcase for their efforts and a way for me to keep them abreast of the latest developments and my current plans. It does take a bit of time that some could argue might be better spent acutally working on more books; but there's got to be a balance, for the readers' sakes. Fanmail is another direct vehicle of communication between and author and his or her public. I get a fair amount, some of it forwarded through Ballantine and some of it sent direct, and so far, I've managed to answer all of it personally. It may take a while, at times, but I think it's important, if a fan takes the time and effort to write, that the author make some kind of response. It's dismal to send off those letters and just have them vanish in the abyss. I don't know how long I'll be able to keep up the personal letter answering, but I'm certainly going to try to keep some line of communication open.

JE: For the past several years, you've been an officer and member of the Society for Creative Anachronism. What motivated you to join the organization? Has your association proved enlarging in terms of your writing? What programs does the group sponsor? Are you still an active member?

KK: To really explain the Society for Creative Anachronism would take far more time than we have today, but briefly I'll say that it's an educational, non-profit corporation whose function is to re-create the positive aspects of the Middle Ages as they existed in western Europe. We put on tournaments and feasts and revels, study the various art forms—calligraphy, illumination, music, dance, costuming—and practice them. There are branches in nearly every part of the country, and some outside the continental United States. Part of the idea of the SCA is tied in with the concept called "living history," in which one learns by doing. Most of what I know about medieval fighting techniques, for example, has been learned from watching it in an SCA context. I write ceremonies for the SCA, gleaned from historical research—and then get to actually see them done by real people. Hence, a lot of the pageantry I write about in the books, I've seen and helped stage in the SCA. This is very valuable. When I dedicated *Camber of Culdi* partly to the "good folk of the Society for Creative Anachronism, without whom this book would have been finished far sooner but far less well," I wasn't kidding. I've spent a lot of time with the SCA, but I've also gotten a lot out of it. I feel that it's been a good investment. I've been the equivalent of a Prime Minister or Chancellor; I've been a reigning Princess and Queen; I've been a Herald. I've known the awfulness of watching my champion slain in the lists—and of seeing him win me a crown. I've made and worn clothing of the period. I've cooked medieval meals and produced calligraphed and illuminated scrolls, done galliards and montards and bransles and pavanes and Scottish dances. I've also seen the real devotion of modern-day knights to their vows of chivalry, helped them plan vigils the night before they were to receive the knightly accolade, sat on a grim Court of Chivalry called to chastise a knight who had not lived up to his vows in the SCA contest. I've also made medieval bardings for my horse and tilted at rings and the quintain, though I've never jousted at a human opponent. (The SPCA doesn't approve, and the horses aren't crazy about it, either.) All of these experiences have enriched my existence and made me better able to write about these things.

JE: Asked about the chief differences between male and female fantasy writers, you contend that the best epic fantasy today is being written by women. What accounts for this fact? Which writers come readily to mind? Is there a major difference in the kind of fantasy being written by women as opposed to men?

KK: I can't explain why the best fantasy is currently being written by women. It's simply been my observation that this is true, at least for the kind of fantasy I like to read. One can start with Anne McCaffrey and Andre Norton, go on with Patricia McKillip and Tanith Lee and C. J. Cherryh and Marion Zimmer Bradley, and wind up with a new writer, like Nancy Springer. Some of these women also write science fiction, or mix science fiction and fantasy, but their common point is that they all write good fantasy. I should also mention Mary Stewart and Evangeline Walton, of course; and I've undoubtedly left out some important ones. I think, perhaps, that women tend to be more intuitive, as opposed to being hard-science oriented—more concerned with people rather than things and events; and perhaps it's this which gives us a slight edge in writing the kind of fantasy I enjoy. Notice that I qualify good fantasy as the kind that *I* enjoy, which is entirely subjective. But that's what counts in reading tastes, in the long run. Sometimes one can tell why one likes a particular work; sometimes one can't—but one can almost always say whether one likes or doesn't like it. It's greatly a matter of personal taste. Not that I don't like and admire some of my male colleagues, like Poul Anderson—far from it. But some of the things most hyped in the past have been things I've enjoyed the least—and they have tended to be written by men. I can't explain the correlation.

JE: Finally, what plans do you have for the Deryni series in the future? Will it continue to expand indefinitely? Do you see an end-point in sight? Will you be disappointed when that end comes?

KK: I have at least another six-to-eight books to do in the Deryni series, though I expect to do some other things along the way, too. And if more ideas come along for more Deryni books, I'll do them too, as long as I continue to enjoy them. In addition to the three-book sequences on Morgan's childhood and origins, and what happens to Morgan and Duncan and Kelson two-to-three years after the first trilogy, I'd like to do a book just about Deryni magic, excerpting all the ceremonies and procedures and going more into the theory and such. I think that could be a very interesting project, and one which I know that a large number of my readers are interested in. There are all kinds of possibilities. I don't see any definite end in sight—partly because that would mean a cessation of the creative processes. When you create a whole world, if you've created it in multiple dimensions, you can't help but have it continue to generate more stories. There's always the question cropping up, of, of, "What happened

then?'' Or, "What happened before that?'' Or, "What about So-and-So?''
The concepts and characters will vary, and the way I look at them, as I grow in
my awareness and in my skill at transmitting that awareness to my readers;
but the possibilities are extensive. I see other, non-Deryni products on the hori-
zon, and perhaps they will eventually take precedence over the Deryni; but if
they do, it will only be because I have grown into other areas of concern, and
have other tales to tell, and other lessons to teach, and other wonders to discover.